The Project Manager's Guide to

LESSONS

LEARNED

Turning Insights into Action for Project Success

Dr. Joshua Cunio

Foreword

I met Dr. Cunio after he had read our research on Behavioral Project Management and the integration of brain science with project management. I've met few who 'get it,' and Josh is one of them. Why do I say he gets it? Because the success of projects is more than just tools and techniques and more about the flow of information to the brain. Project management is a thinking person's game. No amount of technology can change that fact. It is what we do with the information, how we get the information, and how we process it to make decisions that either inhibits or enables a successful project outcome. Before I dive into Dr. Cunio's work here, I want to give a bit more context to the word 'information.' This is a frequently used word and not much value is given to its meaning. Let's dig a little deeper. Most people know that more than half of projects fail their time and budget commitments. This is an awful statistic! Here's the interesting part: these stats are usually attributed to optimistic planning, and optimistic planning is usually attributed to optimism bias. And why wouldn't it be attributed to optimism bias? Seems logical, right? Except, most optimistic plans that result in poor project performance may not necessarily be due to optimism bias. What we've found in our research is that much of poor project performance is due to a lack of information (and sometimes optimism bias as well; it's important to not discount that here). This lack of information is a result of missing data due to time pressure, high cognitive load, low psychological safety, cognitive dissonance, or just plain unavailability of the information to begin with. There are many causes of missing information, but the key here is that in many cases poor project performance is due to optimistic planning in a lot of instances, and that optimistic plan isn't always humans being overly optimistic; they just didn't have all the information needed to make a reliable plan to efficiently deliver.

So how does all this tie into Josh's work? Lessons learned is not just a popular term in project management land. It is bringing forward that information. The information that reduces optimistic planning. The information that can reduce optimism bias itself, in some cases. Lessons learned, in the context of brain science, is a form of debiasing the brain in some ways. When we recognize the concept as a way of turning up the computing power of our brain, we truly start to open the doors to better project performance. In Behavioral Project Management, we like to say it's "The Science of Delivering Dreams," because recognizing the computing and decision-making power of the brain is the first step in delivering the big human endeavors we are striving to complete. Especially since project management is a thinking person's game.

Lessons learned, when done well, can counter the brain's automatic thinking system, counter the effects of time pressure, and challenge confirmation bias. Lessons learned is the oft-forgotten element that can assist in benchmarking and reference class forecasting, another important debiasing technique in estimating. I could go on and on, but I'll let you read about the many attributes of lessons learned for yourself in the chapters that follow.

In closing, I'll simply say that Dr. Cunio gets it!

Dr. Joshua Ramirez, NPPQ, PMP
Chief Executive Officer
Institute for Neuro & Behavioral Project Management

Chapter Index

Chapter Structure

This book is structured to take readers on a journey through the various aspects of lessons learned practices. Each chapter builds on the previous one, gradually deepening the reader's understanding and providing practical insights and tools.

Chapter 1: Introduction
Lays the foundation by explaining the background, importance, and objectives of the book. It introduces the concept of lessons learned, the challenges in implementing these practices, and the book's purpose in bridging the gap between theory and practice.

Chapter 2: The Story of Lessons Learned
Provides a narrative of the evolution and significance of lessons learned in project management, including historical milestones, personal anecdotes, and case studies. This chapter sets the stage for understanding the historical context and ongoing relevance of lessons learned.

Chapter 3: Lessons Learned Frameworks and Methodologies
Introduces the Project Integrated Lessons Learned (PILL) Framework and explains each step in detail. It covers how to systematically capture, analyze, and apply lessons learned, ensuring a structured approach to continuous improvement.

Chapter 4: Evidence-Based Management and Practices
Discusses the role of evidence-based management in lessons learned practices. It highlights how empirical data, and systematic analysis can enhance decision-making and project outcomes, supported by real-life examples and case studies.

Chapter 5: The Role of Organizational Culture

Explores how organizational culture impacts lessons learned and strategies for fostering a learning culture. It emphasizes the importance of leadership, structured processes, and an environment that encourages the open sharing of insights.

Chapter 6: Behavioral Science and Lessons Learned

Examines how behavioral science explains project managers' behaviors regarding lessons learned and supports effective implementation. It addresses cognitive biases such as optimism bias, confirmation bias, and status quo bias, providing strategies to mitigate these influences.

Chapter 7: Practical Applications and Tools

Offers templates, tools, and guidance for implementing lessons learned practices. This chapter provides practical resources, including technology integration and training methods, to help project managers effectively capture and apply lessons learned.

Chapter 8: Lessons Learned and Artificial Intelligence

Explores the integration of artificial intelligence (AI) in enhancing lessons learned practices. It discusses how AI can automate data collection, provide predictive insights, and identify patterns to improve project management.

Chapter 9: Conclusion

Recaps the key points discussed throughout the book, explores future directions for lessons learned practices, and provides a call to action for project managers and organizations to embed these practices into their project management processes.

Why This Book Matters

In an era where project complexity is increasing and the margin for error is shrinking, the ability to learn and adapt is more crucial than ever. This book addresses a vital need in the project management community for a comprehensive, evidence-based guide to lessons learned practices. Whether you are a seasoned project manager or a newcomer to the field, this book will provide you with the insights and tools needed to drive project success through effective lessons learned practices.

Engage with the Content

As you read through this book, I encourage you to reflect on your own experiences with lessons learned. Consider how the principles and practices discussed can be applied in your own projects and organizations. By engaging with the content and actively thinking about how to implement these practices, you will be better equipped to drive continuous improvement and achieve greater project success.

CHAPTER 1

Introduction

Background and Purpose

In the fast-paced world of project management, the ability to learn from past experiences and apply those lessons to future projects is invaluable. Lessons learned practices are critical for continuous improvement, risk mitigation, and enhancing organizational learning. Despite their importance, many organizations struggle to implement effective lessons learned processes. This book aims to provide a comprehensive guide to lessons learned practices, supported by evidence-based management principles, real-life examples, advanced methodologies, and insights from behavioral science.

This book delves into the specifics of establishing a robust lesson learned process, from the initial identification and documentation of lessons to their analysis, dissemination, and application. Integrating these practices into the project management lifecycle can lead to more successful project outcomes, as teams build on previous experiences to improve efficiency, effectiveness, and overall project performance.

MEET ALEX, OUR PROJECT MANAGER

To bring these concepts to life, we'll follow the journey of Alex, a seasoned project manager at a mid-sized technology company. Throughout his career, Alex has faced numerous challenges, from project delays to budget overruns. Determined to improve project outcomes, Alex embarks on a mission to implement effective lessons learned practices within his organization.

With a strong background in project management, Alex understands the theoretical importance of lessons learned but has struggled to effectively put these practices into action. The obstacles Alex faces are common in many organizations: time constraints, limited resources, and a culture that doesn't always support open discussions of failures. Despite these challenges, Alex is committed to fostering a culture of continuous improvement and learning within his team.

Throughout this book, we will follow Alex as he navigates the complexities of implementing lessons learned practices. From capturing insights during project reviews to integrating advanced tools like AI and leveraging behavioral science, Alex's journey provides practical, real-world examples of overcoming common barriers and successfully embedding lessons learned into the project management process. Through Alex's experiences, readers will gain valuable insights and actionable strategies to apply in their own organizations, driving project success and fostering a culture of continuous improvement.

Importance of Lessons Learned in Project Management

Lessons learned are critical for several reasons. They help organizations:

1. **Avoid Repeating Mistakes:** By analyzing past project failures, teams can identify what went wrong and implement strategies to prevent similar issues in future projects. Research by the Project Management Institute (PMI) shows that effective lessons learned practices can reduce project failures by up to 35% (PMI, 2021).

2. **Replicate Successes:** Understanding what worked well in previous projects allows teams to replicate successful practices. A study by Williams (2008) found that organizations actively using lessons learned are more likely to replicate successful project strategies, leading to a 25% increase in project efficiency.

3. **Improve Processes:** Continuous improvement is a hallmark of high-performing organizations. Lessons learned provide a structured approach to identifying areas for process improvement. According to Kerzner (2022), companies that implement robust lessons learned processes see a 30% improvement in project process efficiency.

4. **Enhance Team Performance:** Sharing lessons learned fosters a culture of learning and collaboration, leading to better team performance. A research paper by Turner and Müller (2005) highlights that teams with a strong lesson learned culture show 20% higher performance rates.

5. **Increase Project Success Rates:** Ultimately, effective lessons learned practices lead to higher project success rates, contributing to overall organizational success. The Standish Group's CHAOS Report (2020) indicates that projects with well-documented lessons learned practices have a 50% higher success rate.

The Role of Behavioral Science in Project Management

Behavioral science is integral to project management, providing insights into how cognitive biases and human behavior impact decision-making. Understanding these concepts is crucial for implementing effective lessons learned practices.

Key Behavioral Science Concepts

1. **Cognitive Biases:** Understanding biases such as optimism bias, confirmation bias, and status quo bias that can affect decision-making (Ramirez & De Baets, 2021).

2. **Behavioral Analysis:** Analyzing team dynamics and individual behaviors to identify potential issues early.

3. **Risk Perception and Management:** Exploring how cognitive biases influence risk assessment and decision-making under uncertainty.

ALEX'S JOURNEY WITH BEHAVIORAL SCIENCE

Throughout this book, we will see how Alex applies behavioral science principles to improve lessons learned practices. By understanding and mitigating cognitive biases, Alex can make more informed decisions and foster a culture of continuous improvement within his team.

The Evolution of Lessons Learned Practices

The concept of lessons learned has evolved significantly over time. Initially, lessons learned were captured informally through verbal exchanges and post-project discussions. However, as project management became more structured, so did the methods for capturing and applying lessons learned.

Historical Milestones

Understanding the historical context of lessons learned practices provides valuable insights into their evolution and importance in project management. This section traces the development of these practices from ancient times to the modern era.

Early Practices

In ancient civilizations, lessons learned were often shared orally, passed down from generation to generation. These early practices relied on storytelling and verbal communication to transmit knowledge and experiences.

For example, the Roman military was known for its disciplined approach to documenting and sharing tactical lessons. After battles, Roman commanders would hold debriefing sessions where strategies and outcomes were discussed in detail. These lessons were meticulously recorded and disseminated throughout the ranks to improve future military campaigns. The Romans understood that learning from both victories and defeats was essential for refining their tactics and maintaining their dominance. This practice of capturing and sharing knowledge laid the groundwork for more formalized lessons learned processes in later periods.

Industrial Revolution

During the Industrial Revolution, lessons learned began to be documented more formally, especially in large-scale engineering and manufacturing projects. This period saw the emergence of more systematic approaches to capturing and applying lessons.

The complexity and scale of projects during the Industrial Revolution, such as the construction of railways, bridges, and factories, necessitated a more organized method of managing knowledge. Engineers and project managers began to keep detailed records of their projects, noting what worked well and what didn't. These records were used to improve future projects, ensuring that mistakes were not repeated, and successful strategies were replicated.

For instance, the construction of the London Underground in the 19th century involved significant engineering challenges and innovative solutions. The lessons learned from each phase of the project were documented and used to inform subsequent phases, contributing to the overall success of the project. This era marked a significant shift toward the formalization of lessons learned practices, setting the stage for modern project management methodologies.

Modern Project Management

The introduction of formal project management methodologies like PRINCE2 (Projects IN Controlled Environments) and PMBOK (Project Management Body of Knowledge) emphasized the importance of lessons learned as a critical component of the project lifecycle. These methodologies provide structured frameworks for managing projects, with lessons learned being an integral part of the process.

Organizations began to adopt more structured approaches to capturing and applying lessons. In PRINCE2, for example, lessons learned are captured throughout the project and reviewed at the end of each stage. This ensures that valuable insights are identified and used to inform future stages of the project. Similarly, PMBOK outlines specific processes for capturing, analyzing, and applying lessons learned to improve project performance and organizational learning (PMI, 2021).

The modern approach to lessons learned involves not only capturing what went wrong but also recognizing what went well. This balanced perspective helps organizations build on their successes while avoiding past mistakes. Tools and technologies such as project management software, knowledge management systems, and collaborative platforms have further enhanced the ability to capture and disseminate lessons learned efficiently.

The Digital Age and Beyond

In the digital age, the ability to capture, analyze, and share lessons learned has been greatly enhanced by advances in technology. The use of artificial intelligence (AI) and machine learning (ML) in project management allows for more sophisticated analysis of project data, identifying patterns and insights that might be missed by human analysts.

Collaborative tools and platforms facilitate real-time knowledge sharing across geographically dispersed teams. Cloud-based systems ensure that lessons learned are accessible to all team members, regardless of location. These technological advancements have made the lessons learned process more efficient and effective, enabling organizations to continuously improve their project management practices.

As we move into the future, the integration of behavioral science insights into lessons learned practices will become increasingly important. Understanding how cognitive biases and human behavior impact the way lessons are captured and applied will help organizations create more robust and effective lessons learned processes. This holistic approach will ensure that lessons learned continue to drive continuous improvement and organizational success in an ever-evolving project management landscape.

The Apollo program is a prime example of how lessons learned can be effectively applied. After the tragic Apollo 1 fire in 1967, NASA conducted a thorough investigation and implemented extensive changes based on the lessons learned. These changes significantly improved safety protocols and engineering practices, contributing to the success of subsequent missions, including the historic Apollo 11 moon landing (Murray & Cox, 1989).

Lessons in Engineering and Design

The Apollo program's engineering successes were rooted in meticulous planning and innovative design philosophies. The design of the Apollo spacecraft, particularly its propulsion systems, was influenced by lessons learned from earlier projects such as Mercury and Gemini. These programs provided critical insights into reliability, redundancy, and testing methodologies that were essential for the success of Apollo missions.

According to Owen (2010), the design of the Apollo spacecraft emphasized reliability through extensive development, qualification, and acceptance testing. The propulsion systems, for instance, incorporated redundant components and rigorous quality assurance processes to ensure mission success. This focus on reliability and thorough testing remains a best practice in aerospace engineering and project management today.

Knowledge Management and Documentation

One of the critical lessons from the Apollo program was the importance of effective knowledge management and documentation. NASA's approach to capturing and disseminating knowledge from the Apollo missions laid the groundwork for future projects, such as the Constellation program.

Grabois (2011) notes that NASA's efforts to recapture and make available the lessons learned from Apollo aimed to prevent the "reinventing of the wheel" for future projects. This initiative ensured that knowledge from the Apollo era was accessible to new generations of engineers and managers working on subsequent programs (Grabois, 2011).

Behavioral Science and Team Dynamics

The Apollo program also highlighted the importance of understanding human factors and team dynamics in mission success. The role of behavioral science in project management was evident in how NASA managed cognitive biases and team interactions. Ramirez and De Baets (2021) discuss the impact of cognitive biases, such as optimism bias and risk aversion, on decision-making. Understanding these biases helped NASA develop strategies to mitigate their effects, contributing to more effective project management and mission success (Ramirez & De Baets, 2021).

Crisis Management and Problem-Solving

The Apollo 13 mission serves as a classic example of effective crisis management and problem-solving under extreme pressure. The mission faced a critical failure when an oxygen tank exploded, threatening the lives of the astronauts and the mission's success. Johnson (2020) documents the engineering challenges and the swift, innovative responses that enabled the safe return of the crew. The incident underscored the importance of flexibility, creativity, and rapid decision-making in crisis situations (Johnson, 2020).

Long-Term Impact and Legacy

The legacy of the Apollo program extends beyond its immediate technological achievements. It set a precedent for how large-scale, complex projects should be managed and executed. Seamans and Ordway (1977) highlight the interdisciplinary nature of the Apollo management process, which required integrating political support, funding, manpower, industrial team management, and project visibility. This comprehensive approach ensured that the millions of components involved in the program worked reliably together (Seamans & Ordway, 1977).

The Apollo program's success was not merely a result of advanced technology but also of exceptional project management, knowledge management, and an understanding of human factors. The lessons learned from Apollo continue to inform and inspire current and future space exploration projects, emphasizing the importance of reliability, thorough testing, effective documentation, and crisis management.

CASE STUDY: CONSTRUCTION INDUSTRY

In the construction industry, lessons learned are vital for improving safety, efficiency, and quality. For instance, several major construction firms—Bechtel Corporation, Fluor Corporation, Skanska, and Turner Construction Company— implemented a lessons learned process after experiencing repeated delays and cost overruns on multiple projects. By systematically capturing and analyzing lessons from past projects, they identified common issues such as inadequate planning and poor communication. Applying these insights to future projects resulted in significant improvements in project timelines and budgets (Gibson Jr. et al., 2006).

Importance of Lessons Learned Systems

Lessons learned systems in construction management are crucial for avoiding past mistakes and replicating successful outcomes. These systems enhance a construction company's competitiveness by systematically capturing, storing, and disseminating knowledge gained from previous projects (Arditi et al., 2010).

Despite their potential benefits, the implementation of such systems in the construction industry has often been inadequate, particularly concerning construction management practices (Arditi et al., 2010).

Developing Competency in Project Management

Project managers in the construction industry must adapt to evolving roles and demands. Maintaining professional competency involves acquiring and updating knowledge and skills through continuous training and experience. Edum-Fotwe and Mccaffer (2000) argue that traditional engineering training is insufficient for today's construction project managers, who must also develop broader management skills.

Knowledge Management and Technology Integration

Effective knowledge management is critical in the construction industry, where projects are often dispersed and involve multiple stakeholders. Eken et al. (2020) developed a web-based lessons learned management system, LinCTool, which categorizes and retrieves lessons learned based on project similarities. This system enhances organizational learning by making knowledge easily accessible and usable across different projects (Eken et al., 2020).

Barriers to Effective Knowledge Capture

Despite the benefits, several barriers hinder the effective capture and utilization of lessons learned in the construction industry. Shokri-Ghasabeh and Chileshe (2014) identified key barriers such as a lack of employee time, resources, and clear guidelines. Addressing these barriers requires a structured approach and strong management support (Shokri-Ghasabeh & Chileshe, 2014).

Organizational Learning and Continuous Improvement

Organizational learning is a core competency for construction firms, facilitating continuous improvement of processes and procedures. Caldas et al. (2009)

highlight the importance of lessons learned programs for retaining institutional knowledge and improving project outcomes. Successful programs address multiple aspects, including capturing, storing, and disseminating knowledge effectively (Caldas et al., 2009).

Practical Applications and Success Stories

1. **Improved Project Timelines and Budgets:** Major construction firms such as Bechtel Corporation, Fluor Corporation, Skanska, and Turner Construction Company systematically implemented lessons learned processes after experiencing repeated delays and cost overruns. By identifying and addressing common issues such as inadequate planning and poor communication, these firms achieved significant improvements in project timelines and budgets (Gibson Jr. et al., 2006).

2. **Enhanced Knowledge Sharing:** An Australian study found that larger construction contractors were more aware of the importance of lessons learned documentation and implemented formal procedures for recording and sharing this knowledge. This practice led to better project performance and competitiveness (Shokri-Ghasabeh & Chileshe, 2014).

The construction industry can significantly benefit from robust lessons learned systems that capture, store, and disseminate knowledge effectively. Overcoming barriers such as lack of time, resources, and clear guidelines is essential for maximizing the potential of these systems. By fostering a culture of continuous improvement and leveraging technology, construction firms can enhance their project management practices and overall competitiveness.

Challenges in Implementing Lessons Learned

Despite the clear benefits, many organizations face challenges in implementing effective lessons learned practices. Common obstacles include:

1. **Lack of Time:** Project teams often prioritize immediate project demands over long-term learning, leading to a "check-the-box" approach to lessons learned. Time constraints and pressure to meet deadlines can result in superficial reviews rather than in-depth analysis of what was learned during the project. According to a study by Duffield and Whitty (2015), project teams frequently struggle to allocate sufficient time for thorough lessons learned sessions, which undermines the potential benefits of the process.

2. **Resistance to Change:** Team members may be reluctant to adopt new processes or share their experiences, especially if they perceive it as a threat to their job security or reputation. Resistance to change is a well-documented phenomenon in organizational behavior, and it can significantly hinder the effective implementation of lessons learned practices. Kotter (1996) highlights that employees' fear of negative consequences can prevent them from openly discussing failures or embracing new methodologies. Overcoming this resistance requires fostering a culture of trust and psychological safety, where team members feel comfortable sharing their insights without fear of retribution.

3. **Inadequate Processes:** Without a structured approach, lessons learned can be haphazardly captured and easily forgotten. An unstructured or informal process can lead to inconsistent documentation, making it difficult to retrieve and apply lessons in future projects. According to Williams (2008), the lack of a systematic framework for capturing and analyzing lessons learned is a common barrier to their effective use. Organizations need clear guidelines and standardized procedures to ensure that lessons are systematically recorded, analyzed, and disseminated.

4. **Insufficient Leadership Support:** Successful implementation of lessons learned practices requires strong support from organizational leaders. Leadership commitment is crucial for fostering a culture that values continuous improvement and learning. Leaders play a key role in championing lessons learned initiatives, allocating necessary resources, and reinforcing the importance of these practices. Research by Kerzner (2022) indicates that projects are more likely to benefit from lessons learned when senior management actively supports and participates in the process. Without leadership endorsement, lessons learned practices may lack the necessary authority and visibility to be effective.

Behavioral Science Insights

Behavioral science provides valuable insights into the cognitive biases that can affect project management practices. By understanding and addressing these biases, project managers can improve decision-making and enhance the effectiveness of lessons learned practices.

Optimism Bias

Project managers often underestimate risks and overestimate the likelihood of success. This bias can lead to unrealistic project plans and a lack of preparedness for potential challenges. Mitigating this bias involves providing data-driven predictions and risk assessments. By relying on empirical data and historical project performance, managers can develop more accurate forecasts and contingency plans. Ramirez and De Baets (2021) suggest using predictive analytics and scenario planning tools to present a more balanced view of potential project outcomes, helping teams prepare for a range of scenarios rather than just the most optimistic one.

Anchoring Bias

Anchoring bias refers to the tendency to rely too heavily on the first piece of information encountered when making decisions. This initial "anchor" can significantly skew judgment and lead to suboptimal project outcomes For example, a project team might base budget estimates on the first figure proposed during a planning session, even if subsequent analysis reveals it to be unrealistic or incomplete. This bias can restrict flexibility and hinder the adoption of more accurate assessments.

Mitigating anchoring bias involves deliberate strategies, such as encouraging multiple initial estimates, using data-driven benchmarks, and fostering an environment where assumptions are regularly challenged. Ramirez and De Baets (2021) emphasize the importance of structured frameworks that allow team to recalibrate their expectations as new information emerges. By actively addressing this bias, project managers can enhance their decision-making accuracy and promote a more adaptive approach to planning and execution.

Confirmation Bias

Teams may focus on information that confirms their pre-existing beliefs while ignoring contradictory evidence. This bias can lead to poor decision-making and missed opportunities for improvement. To counteract confirmation bias, analytical tools can be employed to highlight discrepancies and encourage objective analysis. Ramirez and De Baets (2021) recommend using decision support systems and structured review processes that require teams to consider alternative viewpoints and conflicting data. By fostering a culture of critical thinking and open discussion, project managers can ensure that decisions are based on a comprehensive evaluation of all available evidence.

Status Quo Bias

Resistance to change can hinder the adoption of new practices and innovations. This bias is often rooted in a preference for maintaining current practices, even when they are suboptimal. Understanding team dynamics and suggesting strategies to overcome inertia is crucial for fostering a culture of continuous improvement. Ramirez and De Baets (2021) emphasize the importance of change management techniques, such as involving team members in the development of new processes, providing clear rationales for changes, and offering training and support to ease transitions. By actively addressing the psychological barriers to change, project managers can encourage their teams to embrace new practices and continuously seek better ways of working.

Alex's Experience: Alex encountered resistance when introducing new lessons learned processes. By applying principles from behavioral science, Alex was able to provide empirical evidence of the benefits, addressing cognitive biases and gaining team buy-in. Behavioral analysis helped Alex better understand team dynamics and implement strategies to foster a culture of learning and improvement.

Addressing These Challenges

To overcome these challenges, organizations need to foster a culture that values continuous learning and improvement. Key strategies include:

1. **Strong Leadership:** Leaders who champion the lessons learned process and lead by example can significantly influence its adoption and effectiveness. Leadership commitment is crucial for creating an environment where lessons learned are prioritized and valued. When leaders actively participate in lessons learned sessions and demonstrate their importance through their actions, they set a precedent for the rest of the organization. According to

Kotter (1996), transformational leaders who advocate for change and foster a learning culture are more likely to successfully implement new processes. Leaders should also ensure that adequate resources are allocated to support lessons learned activities, reinforcing their commitment to continuous improvement.

2. **Formal Processes:** Implementing structured frameworks like the Project Integrated Lessons Learned (PILL) Framework™, developed by Dr. Cunio, ensures that lessons are systematically captured, analyzed, and applied. Formal processes provide clear guidelines and standardized procedures, reducing the likelihood of lessons being overlooked or inconsistently documented. Duffield and Whitty (2015) highlight that a systematic approach to lessons learned, supported by a robust framework, helps organizations institutionalize these practices and integrate them into the project lifecycle. Structured frameworks also facilitate the consistent application of lessons across projects, enhancing organizational learning and performance.

3. **Technology Integration:** Leveraging technology to capture, store, and disseminate lessons learned can enhance accessibility and usability. Knowledge management systems, collaborative platforms, and project management software can streamline the lessons learned process, making it easier to document insights and share them with relevant stakeholders. Williams (2008) notes that technology can significantly improve the efficiency and effectiveness of lessons learned practices by providing centralized repositories and real-time access to information. Tools such as AI and machine learning can also analyze data to identify patterns and trends, offering deeper insights into project performance.

4. **Regular Training:** Providing regular training and workshops to educate team members on the importance and methods of capturing lessons learned is

essential for building competency and engagement. Training programs should cover the principles of lessons learned, the use of relevant tools and frameworks, and techniques for effective knowledge sharing. Senge (2006) emphasizes that continuous learning and professional development are key components of a learning organization. Regular training ensures that team members are equipped with the skills and knowledge needed to contribute to the lessons learned process, fostering a culture of continuous improvement.

ALEX'S JOURNEY BEGINS

As we follow Alex's journey, we will see how he encounters and overcomes these challenges in his quest to implement effective lessons learned practices. Through Alex's experiences and the integration of behavioral science insights, we will explore practical applications of the concepts discussed in each chapter, providing a relatable and engaging narrative that illustrates the real- world impact of lessons learned.

Chapter Insights

_____

_____

_____

_____

_____

_____

_____

_____

_____

_____

_____

_____

_____

_____

_____

_____

_____

CHAPTER 2
The Story of Lessons Learned

Introduction to Alex's Journey

Alex, a seasoned project manager at a mid-sized technology company, has faced numerous challenges throughout his career, from project delays to budget overruns. Determined to improve project outcomes, Alex embarks on a mission to implement effective lessons learned practices within his organization. This chapter follows Alex's journey, illustrating the evolution and significance of lessons learned in project management through real-life examples, case studies, and personal anecdotes.

During a particularly challenging project, Alex realized the value of documenting lessons learned when a recurring issue led to significant delays. This experience was a turning point, motivating Alex to champion a more structured approach to capturing and applying lessons learned. Alex began to recognize the importance of not just identifying issues but also understanding their root causes and sharing these insights with the team to prevent future occurrences.

Historical Context

The practice of capturing lessons learned has roots in various disciplines, including military strategy, engineering, and management sciences. In project management, the formalization of lessons learned practices can be traced back to the late 20th century when organizations began to systematically capture and apply insights from completed projects.

In ancient civilizations, lessons learned were often shared orally and passed down through generations. The Roman military, for example, documented and shared tactical lessons to improve their strategies. This practice of systematically capturing and disseminating knowledge laid the foundation for more structured approaches in later periods. Military history provides valuable metaphors for management, which, when studied carefully, offer profound insights for contemporary project management (Ahlstrom et al., 2009).

Industrial Revolution

During the Industrial Revolution, the complexity of large-scale engineering projects, such as the construction of railways, bridges, and factories, necessitated a more systematic approach to capturing and applying lessons. This period saw the emergence of practices focused on improving safety, efficiency, and overall project success. The engineering feats of this era required rigorous documentation and analysis to ensure project outcomes could be replicated and improved upon. The systematic approaches developed during this time laid the groundwork for modern project management methodologies (Godoy, 2011).

Modern Project Management

The formalization of project management methodologies in the late 20th century significantly advanced the practice of capturing lessons learned. The introduction of methodologies such as PRINCE2 and the PMBOK emphasized the importance of lessons learned as a critical component of the project lifecycle. These methodologies provided structured approaches for documenting and applying lessons to improve future project outcomes (PMI, 2021).

Table 2.1: Historical Milestones of Lessons Learned

Period	Milestone	Description
Ancient Civilization	Oral Traditions	Knowledge passed down through generations
Industrial Revolution	Form Documentation	Systematic approaches to capturing lessons
Modern Era	Project Management Frameworks	Introduction of structured methodologies like PMBOK and PRINCE2

Lessons from Military Strategy

The field of military strategy offers valuable lessons for project management. Ancient military strategies, such as those from the Roman Empire and other historical contexts, have been adapted to modern management practices. For example, the principles of leadership and strategic planning in ancient Thai military history have been correlated with modern construction project management processes. This demonstrates how historical military strategies can enhance leadership qualities in contemporary project management (Sui & Chuvessiriporn, 1997).

Organizational Learning and Systemic Models

Recent advancements in project management have introduced systemic models to enhance the lessons learned process. Duffield and Whitty (2015) proposed adapting the Swiss cheese model, traditionally used in healthcare and aviation, to enable project organizations to conceptualize and implement effective lessons learned practices. This model integrates elements such as individual learning, culture, social interactions, technology, process, and infrastructure to promote comprehensive organizational learning (Duffield & Whitty, 2015).

Historical Perspectives on Project Management Models

Understanding the historical development of project management models is crucial for appreciating their current applications. Garel (2013) highlighted the evolution from pre-models of project management to the standard North American model. This historical trajectory emphasizes the transition from ad hoc practices to formalized, systematic approaches that are widely used today (Garel, 2013).

CASE STUDY: NASA'S APOLLO PROGRAM

The Apollo program is a prime example of how lessons learned can be effectively applied. After the tragic Apollo 1 fire in 1967, NASA conducted an extensive investigation and applied the lessons learned to improve safety protocols and engineering practices. This meticulous approach contributed significantly to the success of subsequent missions, including the historic Apollo 11 moon landing (Murray & Cox, 1989).

ALEX'S FIRST ENCOUNTER WITH LESSONS LEARNED

Early in Alex's career, he was part of a high-stakes software development project that ultimately failed due to repeated mistakes and overlooked risks. This experience underscored the importance of systematically capturing and applying lessons learned. Determined to avoid similar pitfalls in the future, Alex began exploring various methods and frameworks for lessons learned.

Personal Anecdote: The Failed Project

Alex recalls the moment when the project was declared a failure. The team had missed critical deadlines, and the final product was riddled with defects. In the post-mortem meeting, it became clear that many of the issues could have been avoided if past lessons had been documented and applied. This turning point motivated Alex to champion lessons learned practices within his organization.

The Evolution of Alex's Approach

Alex started by implementing informal debriefings and retrospective meetings. However, he quickly realized that a more structured approach was needed to capture meaningful insights and ensure they were applied to future projects. This led Alex to research and adopt the Project Integrated Lessons Learned (PILL) Framework, which provided a comprehensive and systematic method for capturing, analyzing, and applying lessons learned.

Challenges and Successes

Implementing lessons learned practices can be fraught with challenges, but overcoming these obstacles can lead to significant improvements in project outcomes. Here are some common challenges faced and strategies used to address them:

Common Challenges

1. Resistance to Change

◇ **Description:** Team members were initially reluctant to adopt new processes, viewing them as additional work. This resistance often stemmed from a lack of understanding of the value of lessons learned and a fear of being blamed for past mistakes.

◇ **Strategy to Overcome:** To address this, Alex held workshops to explain the benefits of lessons learned and how they contribute to continuous improvement. By creating a safe environment where team members felt comfortable sharing their experiences without fear of blame, Alex gradually increased buy-in. Involving team members in developing the lessons learned process also helped reduce resistance.

2. Lack of Time

◊ **Description:** The fast-paced nature of projects often led to a "check-the-box" approach to lessons learned, where insights were not fully explored or documented. Project teams were under pressure to move quickly to the next task, leaving little time for reflection.

◊ **Strategy to Overcome:** Alex implemented short, regular debrief sessions at the end of each project phase instead of waiting until project completion. These sessions allowed for timely reflection and documentation of lessons while the experiences were still fresh. Additionally, integrating lessons learned activities into the project schedule as a mandatory component helped ensure that time was allocated for these important reflections.

3. Inconsistent Application

◊ **Description:** Without a formal process, lessons learned were captured haphazardly and rarely applied to future projects. This inconsistency meant that valuable insights were often lost or not utilized effectively.

◊ **Strategy to Overcome:** Alex introduced the Project Integrated Lessons Learned (PILL) Framework™, providing a structured approach to capturing, analyzing, and applying lessons learned. The framework included standardized templates and procedures to ensure consistency. Alex also established a central knowledge repository where all lessons learned were stored and made accessible to the entire organization. This repository facilitated easy retrieval and application of lessons to new projects.

By addressing these challenges with targeted strategies, Alex's organization experienced several successes:

1. **Improved Project Outcomes:** The systematic approach to capturing and applying lessons learned led to better project planning, risk management, and overall project performance.

2. **Enhanced Team Collaboration:** The lessons learned process fostered a culture of open communication and continuous improvement, enhancing collaboration among team members.

3. **Organizational Learning:** The centralized knowledge repository became a valuable resource for the organization, contributing to a collective learning culture and reducing the likelihood of repeating past mistakes.

These successes demonstrate the tangible benefits of overcoming common challenges associated with implementing lessons learned practices. By fostering a culture that values continuous learning and improvement, organizations can achieve significant enhancements in project outcomes and organizational effectiveness.

Behavioral Science Insights

◊ **Optimism Bias:** Project managers often underestimate risks and overestimate the likelihood of success. Understanding and mitigating this bias helped Alex approach lessons learned with a more realistic perspective (Ramirez & De Baets, 2021).

◊ **Confirmation Bias:** Teams may focus on information that confirms their beliefs while ignoring contradictory evidence. Alex used analytical tools to highlight discrepancies and encourage objective analysis (Ramirez & De Baets, 2021).

◊ **Status Quo Bias:** Resistance to change can hinder the adoption of new practices. By understanding team dynamics and suggesting strategies to overcome inertia, Alex fostered a culture of continuous improvement (Ramirez & De Baets, 2021).

Overcoming Challenges

1. **Building a Learning Culture:** Alex worked with leadership to foster a culture that valued continuous improvement and learning. They emphasized the long-term benefits of lessons learned practices, such as improved project outcomes and reduced risks.

2. **Implementing Structured Frameworks:** The PILL Framework provided a structured approach to capturing, analyzing, and applying lessons learned. This helped standardize the process and ensure consistency.

3. **Leveraging Technology:** Alex introduced project management tools and knowledge management systems to streamline the documentation and dissemination of lessons learned.

Succes Stories

1. **Improved Project Outcomes:** By systematically applying lessons learned, Alex's team reduced project delays and cost overruns. For example, in one project, they identified and mitigated a critical risk early on, preventing a major setback.

2. **Enhanced Team Performance:** Regular debriefings and retrospective meetings fostered open communication and collaboration, leading to higher team morale and performance.

3. **Organizational Benefits:** The organization benefited from the improved efficiency and effectiveness of project management practices. Lessons learned were shared across teams, leading to better overall project success rates.

REAL-LIFE EXAMPLE: THE CONSTRUCTION INDUSTRY

In the construction industry, lessons learned are vital for improving safety, efficiency, and quality. Construction projects often involve complex coordination among various stakeholders, tight deadlines, and significant risks. By systematically capturing and analyzing lessons from past projects, construction firms can address recurring issues and enhance overall project performance.

For instance, a major construction firm implemented a comprehensive lessons learned process after experiencing repeated delays and cost overruns on several high-profile projects. The firm conducted thorough post-project reviews, gathering input from all team members and stakeholders. They used structured templates to ensure consistency in capturing lessons and held workshops to discuss findings and brainstorm solutions.

Through this process, the firm identified several common issues:

1. **Inadequate Planning:** Many projects suffered from unrealistic timelines and underestimated resource requirements. By understanding the root causes of

these planning failures, the firm developed more accurate project plans and schedules.

2. **Poor Communication:** Miscommunication between project teams and subcontractors often led to delays and rework. The firm implemented regular communication protocols and check-ins to ensure that everyone was aligned and informed throughout the project lifecycle.

3. **Safety Concerns:** Recurring safety incidents highlighted the need for better training and adherence to safety protocols. The firm introduced comprehensive safety training programs and stricter enforcement of safety measures.

By applying these insights to future projects, the firm saw significant improvements in project timelines and budgets. For example:

◊ **Project Timelines:** Enhanced planning and communication reduced delays, allowing projects to be completed on or ahead of schedule. This improvement not only saved time but also minimized the financial impact of project delays.

◊ **Budgets:** Better resource estimation and management led to more accurate budgeting and reduced cost overruns. The firm was able to allocate resources more efficiently and avoid unnecessary expenses.

◊ **Safety:** The emphasis on safety training and protocols led to a noticeable decrease in safety incidents, creating a safer working environment for all employees.

These improvements were documented and shared across the organization, fostering a culture of continuous learning and improvement. The success of the lessons learned process in the construction firm demonstrates the value of systematically capturing, analyzing, and applying lessons to enhance project outcomes and drive organizational success (Gibson Jr. et al., 2006).

By leveraging the insights gained from past projects, the construction firm not only improved its project execution but also built a foundation for sustained excellence and innovation in its operations.

 **REAL-LIFE EXAMPLE: IT PROJECTS**

In the IT sector, lessons learned are crucial for enhancing product quality, customer satisfaction, and overall project success. IT projects often involve complex systems, tight deadlines, and rapidly changing requirements, making it essential to continuously improve processes and practices through systematic lessons learned.

A global software company faced significant challenges with their product launches due to recurring bugs and high levels of customer dissatisfaction. These issues were negatively impacting the company's reputation and financial performance. To address these challenges, the company decided to establish a formal lessons learned process.

The process involved several key steps:

1. **Post-Launch Reviews:** After each product launch, the company conducted detailed post-launch reviews to capture feedback from development teams, testers, and customers. These reviews were structured to ensure comprehensive coverage of all aspects of the project.

2. **Root Cause Analysis:** The company used root cause analysis techniques to identify the underlying causes of recurring bugs and customer complaints. This analysis revealed critical issues such as insufficient testing and unclear requirements.

3. **Collaborative Workshops:** Cross-functional workshops were held to discuss the findings from the post-launch reviews and root cause analysis. These workshops brought together developers, testers, project managers, and customer support teams to brainstorm solutions and share best practices.

Through this structured approach, the company identified several key areas for improvement:

1. **Insufficient Testing:** The analysis revealed that many bugs were due to inadequate testing during the development phase. To address this, the company introduced more rigorous testing protocols, including automated testing tools and comprehensive test coverage plans. These protocols ensured that software was thoroughly tested before release, reducing the likelihood of post-launch bugs.

2. **Unclear Requirements:** Unclear and frequently changing requirements were leading to misunderstandings and misalignments between teams. The company established clearer communication channels and standardized requirement documentation processes. Regular meetings between developers, product managers, and stakeholders ensured that everyone had a shared understanding of project requirements, and any changes were communicated promptly.

As a result of these improvements, the company experienced more successful product launches:

◊ **Reduction in Bugs:** The introduction of rigorous testing protocols significantly reduced the number of bugs found in released products. This improvement not only enhanced product quality but also boosted customer satisfaction.

◊ **Clearer Communication:** Enhanced communication channels and standardized documentation processes led to better alignment between teams, reducing misunderstandings and improving overall project coordination.

◊ **Customer Satisfaction:** With fewer bugs and more reliable products, customer satisfaction increased. Positive customer feedback and fewer support requests reflected the success of the improvements made.

These successes were documented and shared across the organization, creating a repository of best practices and lessons learned. This repository became a valuable resource for future projects, ensuring that the insights gained were applied consistently across all teams and projects.

By establishing a formal lessons learned process, the global software company systematically identified and addressed the root causes of their challenges, leading to more successful product launches and higher customer satisfaction (Williams, 2008). This example highlights the importance of a structured approach to capturing, analyzing, and applying lessons learned in the IT sector, driving continuous improvement and project success.

Conclusion

The journey of lessons learned in project management is a testament to the power of continuous improvement. By learning from past experiences, organizations can avoid repeating mistakes, replicate successes, and ultimately enhance their project outcomes. Alex's story illustrates the transformative potential of lessons learned practices when implemented effectively.

Alex's initial challenges highlight common obstacles many organizations face, such as resistance to change and the lack of structured processes. However, Alex's perseverance and commitment to fostering a learning culture demonstrate that these challenges can be overcome. By actively engaging team members, encouraging open communication, and leveraging structured approaches, Alex was able to turn lessons learned from a theoretical concept into a practical, impactful tool.

As Alex navigated through various projects, it became clear that the benefits of lessons learned extend beyond immediate project improvements. They contribute to building a resilient organization capable of adapting to change and continuously evolving. Each lesson learned became a steppingstone toward greater efficiency, innovation, and project success.

Alex's journey also underscores the importance of leadership support in promoting and sustaining lessons learned practices. By gaining buy-in from leadership and demonstrating quick wins, Alex was able to embed these practices into the organizational culture, ensuring their longevity and effectiveness.

As we move forward, the next chapter will delve into the specific frameworks and methodologies for capturing and applying lessons learned. It will provide a detailed guide to implementing these practices in your organization, drawing on both Alex's experiences and established best practices. You will learn about the Project Integrated Lessons Learned (PILL) Framework and other methodologies that can help you systematically capture, analyze, and apply lessons learned to drive continuous improvement in your projects.

By integrating these frameworks into your project management processes, you can create a culture of learning and innovation that not only enhances project outcomes but also contributes to the overall success and sustainability of your organization.

Alex's story is just the beginning, and the tools and insights in the upcoming chapters will equip you with the knowledge and skills to embark on your journey of continuous improvement.

Chapter Insights

_____

_____

_____

_____

_____

_____

_____

_____

_____

_____

_____

_____

_____

_____

_____

_____

CHAPTER 3

Lessons Learned Frameworks and Methodologies

Introduction to Lessons Learned Frameworks

To effectively capture and apply lessons learned, organizations need a structured approach. Frameworks and methodologies provide the necessary structure to ensure that lessons learned are systematically identified, documented, analyzed, and disseminated. This chapter introduces the Project Integrated Lessons Learned (PILL) Framework, developed by Dr. Cunio, along with other methodologies that can be tailored to different project environments.

The Project Integrated Lessons Learned (PILL) Framework™

The PILL Framework is a comprehensive approach designed to integrate lessons learned into every phase of a project lifecycle. It provides a systematic process for identifying, capturing, analyzing, prioritizing, documenting, converting, disseminating, and closing lessons learned. Let's follow Alex as he implements the PILL Framework in his organization.

Review

This step begins in parallel with Project Initiation, regardless of the approach (phased or project-based) used. As soon as a project idea is approved, Project Initiation begins. However, there is typically a small window of time between project idea submission and approval. During this time, the Review step should commence. The first action during this period should be a thorough review of the lessons learned repository, focusing on finding any relevant lessons from similar projects. Key factors to consider when reviewing past lessons learned include:

◊ **Relevance:** The lessons should be pertinent to the new project.

◊ **Similarity:** The lessons should be from projects similar in nature to the new project.

◊ **Actionability:** The lessons should be actionable, even if action has not yet been taken.

Identified past lessons learned should be incorporated into the new project plan. This may occur in various ways, such as identifying new Risks, Issues, Opportunities (RIO), adding them to the new project's Action Item Log, or simply providing information that aids in the overall management of the project.

Overview: The initial phase involves recognizing valuable insights from all stages of a project, including successes and failures, with a focus on understanding the 'what' and 'why' behind each outcome.

Techniques:

◊ **After-Action Reviews (AARs):** Conducted after project milestones to discuss what should have happened, what actually happened, and why there were differences.

◊ **Retrospectives:** Sessions held at the end of project phases to reflect on the team's performance and decision-making processes.

◊ **Surveys and Questionnaires:** Distributed to project stakeholders to gather feedback on project execution and outcomes.

◊ **Interviews:** One-on-one or group interviews with project team members and stakeholders to capture in-depth insights.

Alex's Experience: Alex began implementing AARs and retrospectives after every major project milestone. Initially, team members were skeptical, but as they recognized the value of these sessions, participation and enthusiasm grew.

Alex also introduced surveys to gather anonymous feedback, ensuring that everyone felt comfortable sharing their honest opinions.

Behavioral Science Insight: Overcoming Status Quo Bias

Alex noticed that some team members were resistant to change, a common manifestation of status quo bias (Ramirez & De Baets, 2021). By addressing this bias directly and explaining the benefits of change through data-driven insights, Alex gradually shifted those team members' mindsets.

Step 2: Capturing Lessons

Overview: This step involves systematically documenting insights, ensuring that the captured information is clear, concise, and transferable.

Strategies:

◊ **Structured Debriefing Sessions:** Regular sessions with project stakeholders to discuss and document key learnings.
◊ **Documentation Tools:** Standardized forms or software designed for capturing lessons learned to maintain consistency.
◊ **Collaborative Platforms:** Tools that allow team members to record and share insights in real-time.
◊ **Multimedia Recording:** Using various media such as video, audio, or graphic representations to capture the nuanced aspects of lessons learned.

Alex's Experience: Alex used standardized forms to document lessons learned during debriefing sessions. He also implemented a collaborative platform where team members could upload videos and audio recordings of their insights. This multimedia approach helped capture the full context of each lesson.

Behavioral Science Insight: Mitigating Confirmation Bias

During debriefings, Alex encouraged team members to share diverse perspectives, helping to counteract confirmation bias by ensuring that all viewpoints were considered (Ramirez & De Baets, 2021).

Step 3: Analyzing Lessons

Overview: Evaluating the captured lessons to extract the most valuable insights, understanding the underlying causes of outcomes, and determining how these can be applied to future projects.

Process:
◊ **Categorization:** Sorting lessons into categories or themes.
◊ **Root Cause Analysis (RCA):** Techniques like the Five Whys or fishbone (Ishikawa) diagrams.
◊ **Impact Assessment:** Evaluating the consequences of the issues or successes captured.
◊ **Cross-Project Evaluation:** Comparing lessons across different projects to identify common issues or successful strategies.

Alex's Experience: Alex and his team categorized the lessons into themes such as risk management, communication, and resource allocation. They used root cause analysis to dig deeper into the underlying issues and conducted impact assessments to prioritize the most critical lessons.

Behavioral Science Insight: Addressing Optimism Bias

By using data-driven root cause analysis, Alex was able to counteract optimism bias, helping the team develop a more realistic understanding of project challenges and outcomes (Ramirez & De Baets, 2021).

Step 4: Prioritizing Lessons

Overview: Not all lessons will have the same level of impact. Prioritization helps focus on lessons that offer the most significant benefit in terms of efficiency, cost savings, or risk reduction.

Criteria:

◊ **Impact on Project Success:** How significantly a lesson affects project outcomes.

◊ **Frequency of Occurrence:** How often a particular issue or success has been observed.

◊ **Feasibility of Implementation:** How practical it is to apply the lesson.

◊ **Urgency:** The need to address the lesson based on its time sensitivity.

Alex's Experience: Alex developed a scoring system to prioritize lessons based on impact, frequency, feasibility, and urgency. This systematic approach ensured that the most critical lessons were addressed first, leading to more focused and effective improvements.

Step 5: Documenting Lessons

Overview: Creating a formal record of the lessons learned. The documentation should be accessible and organized systematically.

Best Practices:

◊ **Use a Standardized Format:** Ensuring uniformity and ease of understanding (PMI, 2021).

◊ **Be Concise and Clear:** Clearly articulate the lesson, avoiding ambiguity.

◊ **Include Contextual Information:** Providing background information for clarity and context.

◊ **Capture the Essence:** Focusing on the core message of the lesson.

◊ **Recommend Actionable Steps:** Including specific recommendations or actions.

Alex's Experience: Alex standardized the documentation process by creating a comprehensive template, or Lessons Learned Register, that included all necessary information. The lessons were stored in a centralized knowledge repository, making it easy for the team to access and review them.

Step 6: Converting Lessons

Overview: Translating the documented insights into practical elements such as risks, issues, opportunities, or action items.

Classification:

◊ **Risks:** Adding potential pitfalls to the project Risk Register with a mitigation plan.
◊ **Issues:** Addressing immediate problems with resolution strategies.
◊ **Opportunities:** Leveraging positive insights for improvements.
◊ **Action Items:** Specific tasks or steps to be taken as a response to a lesson.

Alex's Experience: Alex integrated the lessons learned into the project management plans by updating the risk registers, issue logs, and action item lists. This ensured that the insights were not just documented but actively used to improve project outcomes.

Step 7: Disseminating Lessons

Overview: Sharing the lessons across the organization to ensure that they benefit more than just the project team.

Methods:

◊ **Internal Reports and Newsletters:** Summaries of lessons learned.

◊ **Knowledge Repositories:** Centralized systems for storing and sharing lessons.

◊ **Workshops and Training Sessions:** Sessions focused on discussing and learning from recent projects.

◊ **Online Platforms and Forums:** Interactive sharing on intranet sites or discussion forums.

Alex's Experience: Alex used internal reports and newsletters to share the lessons learned across the organization. He also organized workshops and training sessions to discuss these lessons in detail and encourage knowledge sharing.

Behavioral Science Insight: Encouraging Knowledge Sharing

By fostering an environment of trust and collaboration, Alex was able to encourage team members to share their insights openly, overcoming barriers to knowledge sharing (Ramirez & De Baets, 2021).

Step 8: Closing Lessons

Overview: Formally concluding the lessons learned process for a specific project or phase.

Process:

◊ **Final Review:** Ensuring all lessons learned have been captured and nothing has been overlooked.

◊ **Validation of Actions Taken:** Confirming that all identified actions are in progress or completed.

◊ **Stakeholder Sign-Off:** Obtaining formal approval from key stakeholders.

◊ **Update Knowledge Repository:** Ensuring all lessons learned are updated in the organization's system.

◊ **Communicate Closure:** Informing relevant parties that the lessons learned process is complete.

◊ **Reflective Analysis:** Assessing the effectiveness of the lessons learned process itself.

Alex's Experience: **Alex conducted a final review of the lessons learned, ensuring that all insights were captured, and actions were validated. He obtained sign-off from key stakeholders and updated the knowledge repository. A reflective analysis was conducted to assess the effectiveness of the lessons learned process and identify areas for improvement.**

Framework Approaches

Phased Approach

Figure 3.1 illustrates a phased approach to implementing the lessons learned framework. This approach is designed for large, complex projects. It allows for the lessons learned lifecycle to be implemented during a phase (e.g., Initiating [I], Planning [P], Executing [E], Closing [C]). For large projects, this approach of breaking down large amounts of information into smaller, manageable pieces can be easier to manage.

Figure 3.1: PILL Phased Approach

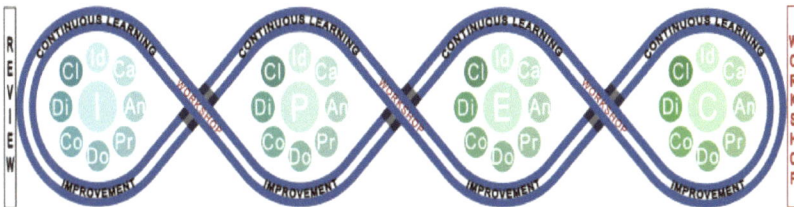

NOTE: This approach is not only designed for the typical project lifecycle phases, but it could be used on how the project is phased or even broken out into workstreams or functional areas.

Project Approach

Figure 3.2 illustrates a holistic project approach to implementing the lessons learned framework, designed for small to medium-sized projects. This approach allows the lessons learned lifecycle to occur in parallel with the project lifecycle.

Figure 3.2: PILL Project Approach

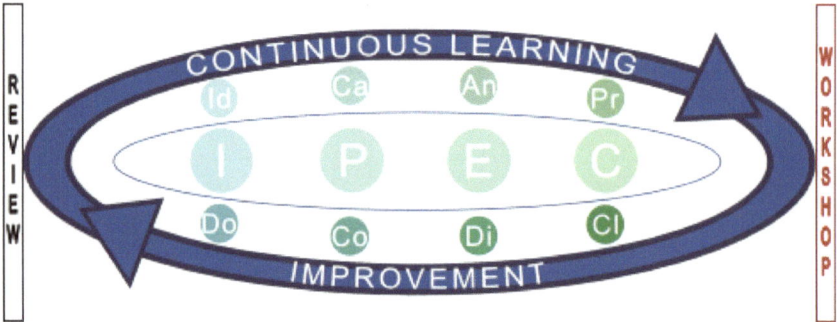

Alex's Experience: When Alex first implemented the PILL Framework, he encountered resistance from team members who were skeptical of its benefits. By demonstrating quick wins and small successes, Alex gradually gained buy-in from the team. For instance, after applying the PILL Framework to a minor project and showcasing tangible improvements in efficiency and problem-solving, the team began to see its value. This incremental approach helped build trust and acceptance of the framework.

Governance and Oversight

Effective governance is crucial for ensuring that lessons learned are consistently captured, analyzed, and applied across projects. The governance structure should include:

- ◊ **Steering Committee:** Comprised of senior management and key stakeholders responsible for setting strategic directions and allocating resources.
- ◊ **PILL Manager:** Oversees the day-to-day operations of the lessons learned process.
- ◊ **Lessons Learned Coordinator:** Captures and documents lessons within projects.
- ◊ **Regular Reviews:** Conducts quarterly reviews to assess the effectiveness of the lessons learned process.
- ◊ **Performance Metrics:** Establishes metrics to measure the impact of the lessons learned process.
- ◊ **Feedback Loops:** Implements mechanisms for gathering and incorporating feedback from stakeholders.

Alex's Experience: **Alex established a steering committee to oversee the lessons learned process. He appointed a PILL Manager and a Lessons Learned Coordinator to ensure the process was carried out effectively. Regular reviews and** performance metrics helped track the impact of the lessons learned process, and feedback loops ensured continuous improvement.

Conclusion

The exploration of frameworks and methodologies for lessons learned in this chapter underscores their critical importance in achieving project management excellence. By adopting structured approaches like the Project Integrated Lessons Learned (PILL) Framework, organizations can systematically capture, analyze, and apply valuable insights, ensuring that each project contributes to continuous improvement.

Alex's experience with implementing the PILL Framework highlights both the challenges and rewards of structured lessons learned practices. Initially encountering resistance from team members, Alex demonstrated the importance of gaining buy-in through quick wins and small successes. By showing tangible benefits early on, Alex was able to gradually build trust and acceptance within the team, offering a practical path forward for other project managers facing similar obstacles.

The PILL Framework and other methodologies discussed in this chapter provide a comprehensive guide for capturing lessons learned. They offer a step-by- step approach that integrates seamlessly with existing project management processes, ensuring that lessons are not only documented but also effectively applied to future projects. This structured approach helps avoid the pitfalls of ad hoc or inconsistent lessons learned practices, providing a reliable foundation for continuous improvement.

Moreover, comparing different frameworks and their respective advantages and disadvantages equips project managers with the knowledge to select the most suitable approach for their organization. Understanding these methodologies allows for a tailored implementation that aligns with organizational needs and project complexities.

As we move forward, the next chapter will delve into the role of evidence-based management and practices in enhancing lessons learned. It will explore how data-driven decision-making can further improve project outcomes, providing practical examples of how project managers like Alex can leverage empirical evidence to support their lessons learned initiatives.

By integrating evidence-based practices with structured frameworks, project managers can ensure that lessons learned are not only comprehensively captured but also effectively applied to drive continuous improvement. This combination of structured approaches and data-driven insights creates a robust foundation for achieving project management excellence and fostering a culture of learning and innovation within the organization.

Alex's journey through the implementation of the PILL Framework serves as a powerful example of how perseverance, strategic planning, and leadership support can transform lessons learned from a theoretical concept into a practical, impactful practice. As you continue to explore the subsequent chapters, you will gain deeper insights and tools to further enhance your lessons learned practices, ensuring that your organization can achieve sustainable success through continuous improvement.

Chapter Insights

_____

_____

_____

_____

_____

_____

_____

_____

_____

_____

_____

_____

_____

_____

_____

_____

_____

CHAPTER 4

Evidence-Based Management and Practices

Introduction to Evidence-Based Management

Evidence-based management (EBM) is an approach that involves making decisions and managing projects based on the best available evidence from multiple sources. It emphasizes the use of empirical data and scientific research to guide managerial decisions rather than relying solely on intuition or past experiences. This chapter explores how EBM supports effective lessons learned practices and how project managers like Alex can leverage EBM to enhance project outcomes.

Principles of Evidence-Based

1. **Empirical Data and Scientific Research:** EBM relies on systematically collected data and findings from rigorous scientific studies to inform decisions. This ensures that management practices are based on proven methods and facts rather than anecdotal evidence or gut feelings (Barends & Rousseau, 2018).

2. **Critical Thinking and Skepticism:** EBM encourages managers to critically evaluate evidence, question assumptions, and remain open to new information. This critical approach helps avoid biases and ensures that decisions are based on the most reliable evidence available (Rousseau, 2006).

3. **Multiple Sources of Evidence:** Effective EBM integrates evidence from multiple sources, including scientific research, organizational data, practitioner expertise, and stakeholder values and concerns. This comprehensive approach ensures that decisions are well-rounded and consider all relevant factors (Briner et al., 2009).

Supporting Effective Lessons Learned Practices

EBM plays a crucial role in supporting effective lessons learned practices by providing a structured framework for capturing, analyzing, and applying lessons:

1. **Systematic Data Collection:** EBM encourages the systematic collection of data throughout the project lifecycle. This includes quantitative data such as project timelines, budgets, and performance metrics, as well as qualitative data from stakeholder interviews and team debriefs. By systematically gathering this information, project managers can build a robust evidence base for identifying lessons learned (Kerzner, 2022).

2. **Rigorous Analysis:** EBM emphasizes rigorous analysis of the collected data to identify patterns, trends, and root causes. Techniques such as root cause analysis, statistical analysis, and data visualization can help project managers uncover insights that might be missed with a more informal approach. This rigorous analysis ensures that lessons learned are based on objective evidence rather than subjective interpretations (Kerzner, 2022).

3. **Application and Dissemination:** EBM supports the application and dissemination of lessons learned by promoting evidence-based recommendations and practices. By leveraging scientific research and empirical data, project managers can develop actionable strategies for addressing identified issues and improving future project outcomes. These strategies can be disseminated through knowledge repositories, training sessions, and organizational policies to ensure widespread adoption and implementation (Barends et al., 2014).

Leveraging EBM to Enhance Project Outcomes

Project managers like Alex can leverage EBM to enhance project outcomes in several ways:

1. **Improved Decision-Making:** By incorporating the best available evidence into decision-making processes, project managers can make more informed and effective decisions. This reduces reliance on intuition and past experiences, which may be biased or outdated, and ensures that decisions are based on

the latest and most reliable information (Pfeffer & Sutton, 2006).

2. **Proactive Risk Management:** EBM allows project managers to proactively identify and mitigate risks based on empirical evidence. By analyzing data from past projects and relevant research, managers can anticipate potential issues and develop strategies to address them before they become critical problems (Kerzner, 2022).

3. **Enhanced Learning and Adaptation:** EBM fosters a culture of continuous learning and adaptation by encouraging project managers to regularly review and update their practices based on new evidence. This iterative approach ensures that lessons learned are continuously integrated into project management processes, leading to ongoing improvements in project performance (Denyer, Tranfield, & van Aken, 2008).

EBM provides a powerful framework for enhancing lessons learned practices and improving project outcomes. By systematically collecting and analyzing data, leveraging scientific research, and integrating evidence from multiple sources, project managers like Alex can make more informed decisions, proactively manage risks, and foster a culture of continuous learning and improvement. This chapter will delve deeper into the principles and applications of EBM, offering practical insights and tools for project managers to implement in their practices.

Definition and Importance

EBM refers to the systematic application of the best available evidence to management decision-making. It involves collecting data, analyzing outcomes, and making informed decisions based on empirical evidence. This approach contrasts with decisions based solely on intuition, personal experience, or conventional wisdom.

EBM involves a structured process that includes the following steps:

1. **Data Collection:** Gathering quantitative and qualitative data from various sources, including past project performance, stakeholder feedback, and industry research.

2. **Data Analysis:** Using statistical tools and analytical methods to identify trends, patterns, and causal relationships within the collected data.

3. **Decision Making:** Making informed decisions that are supported by empirical evidence, ensuring that choices are grounded in reality rather than assumptions.

Figure 4.1: EBM Lifecycle

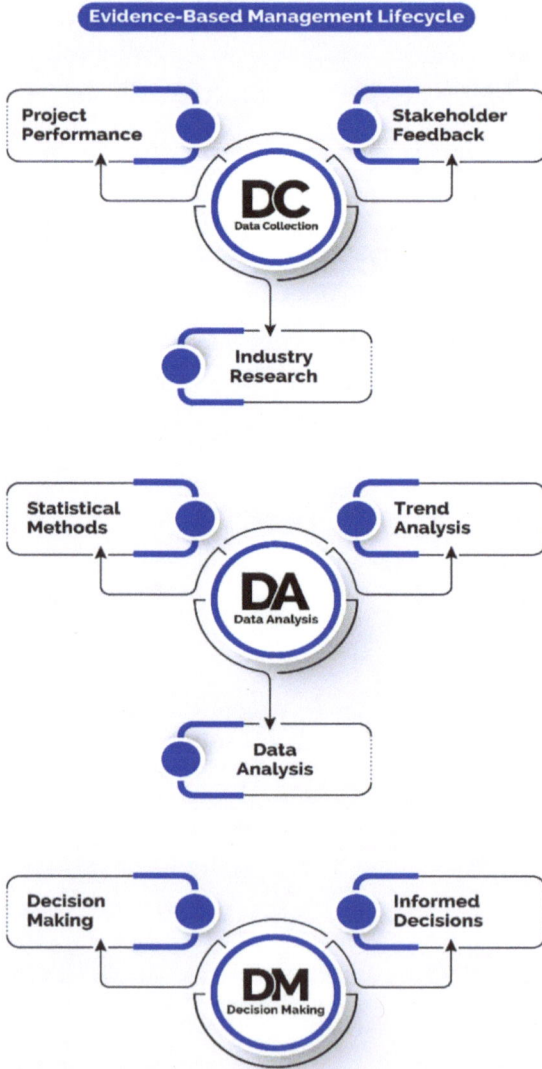

Evidence-Based Management Lifecycle

Project Performance — Stakeholder Feedback — DC Data Collection — Industry Research

Statistical Methods — Trend Analysis — DA Data Analysis — Data Analysis

Decision Making — Informed Decisions — DM Decision Making

Importance

The importance of EBM lies in its ability to improve project outcomes in several key ways:

1. **Reducing Uncertainty:** By relying on empirical data, project managers can make more accurate predictions about project outcomes, thus reducing uncertainty and enhancing planning accuracy (Barends et al., 2015).

2. **Mitigating Risks:** EBM enables the identification and assessment of potential risks based on historical data and research findings. This proactive approach allows for the development of effective risk mitigation strategies (Pfeffer & Sutton, 2006).

3. **Fostering a Culture of Continuous Improvement:** EBM promotes a culture where decisions are continually evaluated and refined based on new evidence. This commitment to learning and adaptation drives ongoing improvements in processes and outcomes (Rousseau, 2006).

4. **Enhancing Credibility and Accountability:** Decisions made using EBM are more transparent and justifiable, enhancing the credibility of management actions and fostering trust among stakeholders (Briner et al., 2009).

By systematically integrating EBM into their practices, project managers like Alex can enhance the reliability and effectiveness of their decisions, leading to better project performance and organizational success.

Application in Project Management

The application of evidence-based management (EBM) in project management involves several key practices that enhance decision-making and improve project outcomes. By systematically collecting and analyzing both quantitative and qualitative data, project managers can make informed decisions that lead to better project performance.

Data Collection and Analysis

1. Quantitative Data:

◊ **Description:** Quantitative data involves collecting numerical information such as project timelines, budgets, and performance metrics. This type of data is crucial for identifying trends and patterns that can inform future projects.

◊ **Example:** Project managers might track the time taken to complete each project phase, budget variances, and resource utilization rates. This data provides objective measures that can be analyzed to understand project performance and identify areas for improvement.

◊ **Reference:** Kerzner (2022) emphasizes the importance of quantitative data in project management, noting that it helps in making data-driven decisions that enhance project efficiency and effectiveness.

2. Qualitative Data:

◊ **Description:** Qualitative data involves gathering descriptive information through methods such as interviews, surveys, and observations. This type of data helps in understanding the context and reasons behind project outcomes, capturing insights that quantitative data might miss.

◊ **Example:** Project managers might conduct post-project interviews with team members to gather feedback on what worked well and what challenges were faced. Surveys can also be used to collect stakeholder opinions on project success and areas for improvement.

◊ **Reference:** Williams (2008) highlights the importance of qualitative insights in project management, arguing that they are essential for capturing the nuances and underlying factors that influence project success.

3. Combining Quantitative and Qualitative Data:

◊ **Integrated Approach:** By combining quantitative and qualitative data, project managers can gain a comprehensive understanding of project performance. Quantitative data provides the "what" and "how much," while qualitative data explains the "why" and "how."

◊ **Benefits:** This integrated approach allows for more robust analysis and decision-making. For example, if a project consistently experiences delays, quantitative data might show the extent of the delays, while qualitative data can provide insights into the root causes, such as communication issues or resource shortages.

◊ **Application:** In practice, project managers can use software tools to collect and analyze both types of data. For instance, project management platforms like Asana or Jira can track quantitative metrics, while feedback can be collected through tools like SurveyMonkey or direct interviews.

By systematically applying these data collection and analysis practices, project managers can enhance their ability to make evidence-based decisions, leading to more successful project outcomes and continuous improvement in project management practices.

CASE STUDY: HEALTHCARE PROJECTS

A study by Barends et al. (2015) highlighted the application of EBM in healthcare projects. By systematically collecting and analyzing data on patient outcomes, project managers were able to identify effective treatments and procedures, leading to improved patient care and reduced costs. This approach aligns with broader trends in healthcare management, emphasizing the importance of EBM and its impact on clinical and operational outcomes.

Evidence-Based Practice in Healthcare

Evidence-based practice (EBP) has been consistently linked to improved quality of care, patient safety, and positive clinical outcomes. A comprehensive review by Connor et al. (2023) revealed that the implementation of EBP in healthcare settings leads to significant improvements in patient outcomes and return on investment (ROI). The review highlighted that EBP practices, particularly in infection prevention and chronic disease management, resulted in reduced hospital stays and lower mortality rates (Connor et al., 2023).

Organizational Culture and EBP

The successful implementation of EBP also depends on the organizational culture and the cognitive beliefs of healthcare professionals. Melnyk et al. (2010) found that healthcare staff's beliefs about the value of EBP were significantly correlated with the extent of its implementation and overall job satisfaction. Hospitals that foster a supportive culture for EBP saw higher levels of staff engagement and better patient care outcomes (Melnyk et al., 2010).

Framework for EBM in Chronic Disease Management

A framework developed by Agnihothri and Agnihothri (2018) for the application of EBM in chronic disease management emphasizes the need for changes in organizational structure, procedures, technology, and provider behaviors. This framework identifies critical areas where managers can implement evidence-based solutions to improve patient outcomes, highlighting the complex interplay between various factors influencing healthcare delivery (Agnihothri & Agnihothri, 2018).

Impact of Evidence-Based Clinical Guidelines

The implementation of evidence-based clinical guidelines has been shown to improve the quality of care. Lugtenberg et al. (2009) conducted a systematic review of Dutch clinical guidelines and found significant improvements in care processes and patient outcomes. The study underscored the need for tailored implementation strategies to maximize the effectiveness of these guidelines in various clinical settings (Lugtenberg et al., 2009).

Case Example: Infection Control in Intensive Care Units

A practical example of EBP's impact is seen in a project aimed at reducing ventilator-associated pneumonia (VAP) and catheter-related bloodstream infections (CRBSI) in an intensive care unit (ICU). Hatler et al. (2006) reported a 54% reduction in VAP and a 78% reduction in CRBSI through the implementation of evidence-based strategies. These improvements not only enhanced patient safety but also resulted in significant cost savings for the healthcare facility (Hatler et al., 2006).

The application of evidence-based management in healthcare projects has demonstrated significant improvements in patient outcomes and operational efficiency. By fostering a culture that supports EBP and implementing systematic frameworks, healthcare organizations can achieve better patient care and reduce costs.

Alex's Experience: In one of Alex's projects, he implemented a data collection strategy that included both quantitative and qualitative data. By analyzing performance metrics and conducting in-depth interviews with team members, Alex was able to identify key issues and opportunities for improvement. This evidence-based approach led to more informed decision-making and better project outcomes.

By leveraging data from past projects, Alex was able to identify patterns that predicted project delays. This insight allowed Alex to implement preemptive measures, significantly improving project timelines.

Systematic Reviews

Conducting systematic reviews of existing research and project data helps identify patterns, trends, and best practices that can inform future projects. Systematic reviews consolidate knowledge and provide a comprehensive understanding of what works and what doesn't (Turner & Müller, 2005).

CASE STUDY: CONSTRUCTION INDUSTRY

In the construction industry, Eken et al. (2020) demonstrated how evidence-based management practices helped a construction firm reduce project delays and cost overruns. By analyzing historical project data, the firm identified common issues and implemented strategies to address them in future projects, resulting in more efficient project execution.

Alex's Experience: Alex conducted systematic reviews of past projects to identify recurring issues and successful strategies. By leveraging this knowledge, Alex was able to implement best practices and avoid common pitfalls in new projects. This systematic approach also helped build a knowledge base that could be referred to for future projects.

Decision-Making Frameworks

Utilizing decision-making frameworks that incorporate empirical evidence, such as risk assessments, cost-benefit analyses, and scenario planning, provides a structured approach to decision-making, ensuring that all relevant factors are considered (Kerzner, 2022).

CASE STUDY: IT PROJECTS

A global IT company used artificial intelligence (AI) to enhance its lessons learned process. The AI system analyzed project data, identifying common issues such as scope creep and communication breakdowns. By providing real-time insights and recommendations, the AI tool helped project managers address these issues proactively. This led to a 20% increase in project success rates and improved client satisfaction.

Managing Scope Creep with AI

AI technologies, such as Bayesian Belief Networks (BBNs), can effectively predict and manage risks like scope creep in software projects. These systems provide insights into potential risks and offer dynamic resource adjustments to mitigate them. Fan and Yu (2004) demonstrated that using BBNs helps maintain the visibility and repeatability of the decision-making process in risk management, thus addressing scope creep efficiently (Fan & Yu, 2004).

Addressing Communication Breakdowns

Effective communication is crucial for managing IT projects. Integrating feedback loops in project management tools can significantly improve communication and project outcomes. Ditt and Schlehofer (1988) developed a project management support tool based on feedback loop techniques, which adapts to project results and improves the support of subsequent projects. This method ensures that communication breakdowns are identified and addressed promptly (Ditt & Schlehofer, 1988).

Benefits of AI in Project Management

AI-powered tools provide real-time insights and predictive analytics that enhance project management efficiency. Trienekens and Kusters (2014) implemented a multi-level feedback loop to improve software project measurement processes. This approach provided project managers with valuable insights into performance metrics, enabling better decision-making and improved project outcomes (Trienekens & Kusters, 2014).

Implementing AI in IT project management enhances the lessons learned process by identifying and addressing common issues such as scope creep and communication breakdowns. This proactive approach leads to improved project success rates and client satisfaction, demonstrating the significant value of AI in managing complex IT projects.

Alex's Experience: Alex adopted decision-making frameworks that integrated empirical evidence into the planning process. For example, by conducting risk assessments based on historical data, Alex was able to anticipate potential issues and develop mitigation strategies. This proactive approach reduced risks and improved project reliability.

Continuous Learning and Adaptation

Implementing a continuous learning process where lessons learned are regularly reviewed and applied to new projects ensures that organizations remain agile and responsive to changing project environments (Ramirez & De Baets, 2021).

CASE STUDY: AEROSPACE INDUSTRY

In the aerospace industry, continuous learning and adaptation are critical for safety and innovation. A study by NASA (2017) highlighted how the organization's rigorous lessons learned process contributed to significant improvements in mission safety and success rates.

Importance of Lessons Learned Processes

NASA's approach to integrating safety, risk management, and assurance processes throughout the project lifecycle has been pivotal. The development of the Process Based Mission Assurance Knowledge Management System (PBMA-KMS) in the late 1990s was a response to challenges posed by fewer prescribed standards and the need for more innovative contracting approaches. This web-based system supports lifecycle safety and mission success management, enabling aerospace professionals to contribute best practices and lessons learned (Newman & Wander, 2002).

Risk Management and Mission Success

Effective risk management is essential for mission success in the aerospace sector. EADS Astrium's Earth Observation and Science Business Unit demonstrated that deploying risk management and lessons learned processes systematically from the proposal phase through development and operations could tailor product assurance programs and activities. This approach has been successful in maintaining high mission success rates while managing costs (Larrere, 2004).

Team Development and Adaptation

Continuous learning extends to team development within NASA's projects. Goodman (2023) noted that identifying lessons learned over a career helps shape engineering decisions and improve team performance. Lessons learned from both human and robotic spaceflight operations highlight the importance of effective team development to ensure mission success and safety (Goodman, 2023). Furthermore, fostering a culture of psychological safety within teams has proven critical. Encouraging open communication and collaboration allows team members to share insights and concerns without fear, leading to enhanced innovation and early identification of risks.

The aerospace industry benefits significantly from structured lessons learned processes. These processes not only enhance mission safety and success rates but also contribute to continuous improvement and innovation within the sector. Incorporating lessons into training programs, operational frameworks, and decision-making models ensures teams remain agile and well-prepared to address evolving challenges and technological advancements.

Alex's Experience: Alex established a continuous learning culture within his team by regularly reviewing lessons learned and incorporating them into new projects. This iterative process helped the team stay updated on best practices and adapt to new challenges effectively. By fostering a culture of continuous improvement,

Alex ensured that the team was always learning and evolving.

Benefits of Evidence-Based Management

The benefits of implementing EBM in project management include:

1. **Improved Decision-Making:** Making informed decisions based on empirical data reduces the likelihood of errors and increases the chances of project success. Evidence-based decisions are more likely to be objective and reliable, as they are grounded in the best available evidence rather than personal biases or untested assumptions. Barends et al. (2014) emphasize that EBM enhances decision quality by relying on the best available evidence.

2. **Enhanced Project Performance:** By continuously learning from past projects and applying evidence-based practices, organizations can improve project performance and outcomes. This approach leads to higher efficiency, better resource utilization, and improved project deliverables. Kerzner (2022) discusses how EBM contributes to improved project performance through systematic learning and application.

3. **Reduced Risks:** Systematic analysis of data helps identify potential risks early, allowing for proactive risk management and mitigation strategies. Early identification and mitigation of risks contribute to smoother project execution and fewer surprises. Williams (2008) highlights the role of data analysis in early risk identification and management.

4. **Increased Stakeholder Confidence:** Evidence-based management fosters transparency and accountability, increasing stakeholders' confidence in project decisions and outcomes. When decisions are backed by data, stakeholders are more likely to trust and support them. Turner & Müller (2005) note that data-driven decision-making enhances stakeholder trust and confidence.

5. **Fostering a Culture of Continuous Improvement:** Organizations that embrace EBM promote a culture of continuous learning and improvement, leading to long-term success and sustainability. This culture encourages innovation, adaptability, and resilience. Ramirez & De Baets (2021) discuss how EBM fosters an environment of continuous improvement and innovation.

Implementing Evidence-Based Management

To effectively implement evidence-based management in project management, organizations can follow these steps:

1. **Establish Clear Objectives:** Define the objectives and goals for implementing EBM practices in the organization. Clear objectives provide direction and focus for EBM initiatives. Kerzner (2022) emphasizes the importance of setting clear objectives for successful EBM implementation.

2. **Develop Data Collection Processes:** Create standardized processes for collecting and analyzing both quantitative and qualitative data. Consistent data collection ensures that the information gathered is reliable and comparable. Williams (2008) outlines the need for standardized data collection processes to support EBM.

3. **Train Project Teams:** Provide training for project teams on the principles and practices of evidence-based management. Training helps build the necessary skills and knowledge for effective EBM implementation. Turner & Müller (2005) highlight the importance of training in building EBM capabilities within project teams.

4. **Utilize Technology:** Leverage technology and software tools to support data collection, analysis, and decision-making processes. Advanced tools can automate data analysis and provide real-time insights. Ramirez & De Baets (2021) discuss the role of technology in enhancing EBM practices through automation and real-time analysis.

5. **Regularly Review and Update Practices:** Conduct regular reviews of EBM practices and update them based on new evidence and changing project needs. Continuous review and adaptation ensure that EBM practices remain relevant and effective. Barends et al. (2014) stress the importance of continuous review and adaptation of EBM practices to maintain their effectiveness.

6. **Engage Stakeholders:** Involve stakeholders in the EBM process to ensure their input and buy-in, fostering a collaborative approach to project management. Stakeholder engagement enhances the relevance and acceptance of EBM practices. Turner & Müller (2005) note the importance of stakeholder engagement in successful EBM implementation.

Conclusion

The integration of evidence-based management (EBM) into lessons learned practices represents a significant advancement in project management. By relying on empirical data and systematic analysis, project managers can make more informed decisions, mitigate risks, and achieve better project outcomes. This chapter has explored the fundamental principles of EBM and demonstrated how these principles can enhance lessons learned practices.

Alex's journey illustrates the transformative impact of adopting an evidence- based approach. By systematically collecting and analyzing data from past projects, Alex identified patterns and trends that informed future decision- making. This data-driven approach not only improved project performance but also fostered a culture of accountability and continuous improvement within the team.

The benefits of EBM are numerous. Improved decision-making, enhanced project performance, reduced risks, and increased stakeholder confidence are just a few of the advantages highlighted in this chapter. By making decisions based on solid evidence rather than intuition or past experiences alone, project managers can achieve more predictable and successful outcomes.

Moreover, the practical examples provided demonstrate how EBM can be seamlessly integrated into existing project management processes. Whether through quantitative data collection, qualitative insights, or advanced analytics, the application of EBM helps project managers like Alex make better-informed decisions and continuously refine their practices.

As we move forward, the next chapter will explore the critical role of organizational culture in the successful implementation of lessons learned practices. It will examine how a supportive culture can facilitate knowledge sharing, foster innovation, and drive continuous improvement. By understanding the interplay between organizational culture and lessons learned, project managers can create an environment that supports sustainable project success.

By combining structured frameworks like the PILL Framework with evidence-based management, project managers can create a robust foundation for capturing and applying lessons learned. This approach ensures that lessons are not only systematically documented but also used to drive tangible improvements in project outcomes.

Alex's experience with EBM serves as a compelling example of how data-driven decision-making can enhance lessons learned practices. By leveraging empirical evidence, project managers can move beyond anecdotal insights and build a more rigorous, reliable foundation for continuous improvement. As you continue to explore the subsequent chapters, you will gain deeper insights and tools to further integrate evidence-based practices into your lessons learned initiatives, ensuring that your organization can achieve sustainable success through continuous learning and adaptation.

In conclusion, the integration of evidence-based management into lessons learned practices offers a powerful approach to enhancing project management capabilities. By grounding decisions in empirical evidence and systematically analyzing project data, organizations can drive continuous improvement, foster a culture of accountability, and achieve better project outcomes. As you apply these principles in your own projects, you will be well-equipped to navigate the complexities of project management and lead your team to greater success.

Chapter Insights

_____

_____

_____

_____

_____

_____

_____

_____

_____

_____

_____

_____

_____

_____

_____

_____

_____

CHAPTER 5

The Role of Organizational Culture

Introduction to Organizational Culture

Organizational culture encompasses the shared values, beliefs, and practices that influence how work is performed and how members of the organization interact. It shapes how employees perceive their roles, responsibilities, and relationships within the organization. This culture is reflected in the company's routines, rituals, language, symbols, and the way decisions are made and communicated.

Organizational culture plays a crucial role in determining how effectively lessons learned are captured, shared, and applied. A positive culture that values continuous learning, openness, and collaboration fosters an environment where lessons learned can thrive. Conversely, a culture resistant to change, secretive, or blame-oriented can hinder the effective implementation of lessons learned practices.

The Role of Organizational Culture in Lessons Learned

1. **Values and Beliefs:** The core values and beliefs of an organization form the foundation of its culture. When these values emphasize the importance of learning and improvement, employees are more likely to engage in lessons learned activities. Organizations that prioritize transparency, accountability, and innovation create fertile ground for capturing and applying lessons learned. For example, companies like Google and Toyota have cultures that encourage continuous learning and improvement, which are integral to their success.

2. **Behavioral Norms and Practices:** Behavioral norms and practices within an organization dictate how employees interact with each other and approach their work. In a culture that supports lessons learned, employees feel safe sharing their experiences, including failures, without fear of blame or retribution. Psychological safety, as described by

Edmondson (1999), is critical for enabling open communication and knowledge sharing. Regular debriefs, team meetings, and feedback sessions become part of the organizational routine, ensuring that lessons are systematically captured and discussed.

3. **Leadership and Role Modeling:** Leaders play a pivotal role in shaping and reinforcing organizational culture. When leaders actively participate in and champion lessons learned practices, they set a positive example for the rest of the organization. Leadership support is crucial for legitimizing these practices and allocating the necessary resources. Leaders who demonstrate a commitment to learning from past experiences and who reward knowledge sharing significantly contribute to fostering a learning culture.

4. **Communication Channels:** Effective communication channels are essential for the dissemination of lessons learned. Organizations need to establish clear and accessible pathways for sharing knowledge, whether through formal reports, meetings, or digital platforms. The use of collaborative tools and knowledge management systems can facilitate real-time sharing of insights and ensure that lessons are accessible to all members of the organization.

5. **Recognition and Rewards:** Recognizing and rewarding employees for their contributions to lessons learned practices can motivate ongoing participation. Organizations can implement recognition programs that highlight individuals or teams who actively engage in capturing and applying lessons learned. Such recognition reinforces the value placed on continuous improvement and encourages others to participate.

1. **Establish Clear Expectations:** Organizations should clearly communicate the importance of lessons learned and set expectations for their capture and application. This involves integrating lessons learned practices into the project lifecycle and making them a standard part of project management processes.

2. **Provide Training and Resources:** Training programs can equip employees with the skills needed to effectively capture, analyze, and apply lessons learned. Providing resources such as templates, guidelines, and access to knowledge management systems supports employees in these activities.

3. **Create Safe Spaces for Sharing:** Fostering an environment where employees feel safe sharing their experiences, including mistakes, without fear of negative consequences is vital. This can be achieved by promoting psychological safety, encouraging open dialogue, and ensuring the focus is on learning rather than blame.

4. **Leverage Technology:** Utilizing technology to support lessons learned practices can enhance their effectiveness. Knowledge management systems, collaborative platforms, and data analytics tools can facilitate the collection, storage, and analysis of lessons learned, making them easily accessible and actionable.

5. **Lead by Example:** Leaders should actively engage in lessons learned activities and model the desired behaviors. By demonstrating a commitment to continuous learning and improvement, leaders can influence the broader organizational culture and encourage others to follow suit.

Impact on Lessons Learned

The impact of organizational culture on lessons learned is profound. It influences how team members perceive the value of lessons learned, their willingness to share experiences, and the overall effectiveness of the lessons learned process. Key aspects include:

1. **Openness to Learning:** Organizations that encourage curiosity, continuous learning, and open discussion of failures and successes are more likely to implement effective lessons learned practices. According to Senge (2006), a learning organization is one that is continually expanding its capacity to create its future. This openness to learning creates an environment where team members feel safe discussing what went wrong and what went right, leading to richer and more actionable lessons learned.

Alex's Experience: Alex fostered a culture of openness by encouraging team members to share both successes and failures during regular team meetings. This approach not only built trust but also led to more innovative solutions.

By creating a safe space where team members felt comfortable discussing their experiences without fear of blame, Alex was able to uncover valuable insights that might have otherwise been overlooked. This openness and transparency contributed to a more collaborative and proactive project environment.

2. **Knowledge Sharing:** A culture that promotes knowledge sharing and collaboration facilitates the dissemination and application of lessons learned across different projects and teams. Nonaka & Takeuchi (1995)

emphasize that knowledge creation and sharing are at the heart of organizational innovation. When team members are encouraged to share knowledge, it becomes easier to apply lessons learned to new projects, thus preventing the repetition of past mistakes and leveraging past successes.

3. **Risk Tolerance:** Cultures that tolerate and learn from risks and failures are more likely to effectively capture and utilize lessons learned, seeing them as opportunities for growth rather than just mistakes. Edmondson (1999) describes psychological safety as a key component of a learning culture, where employees feel safe to take risks and make mistakes. Organizations with higher risk tolerance and a positive attitude towards learning from failures have more robust lessons learned processes, as employees are more willing to report and analyze mistakes.

4. **Leadership Support:** The support and involvement of leadership in promoting and valuing the lessons learned process are critical for its success. Leadership sets the tone for how the organization views and uses lessons learned. Kotter (1996) argues that transformational leadership is essential for driving change and fostering a learning culture. Leaders who actively participate in lessons learned activities and communicate their importance are able to foster a culture that values continuous improvement.

5. **Employee Empowerment:** Cultures that empower employees to contribute to and implement lessons learned encourage a more engaged and proactive approach to project management. Thomas & Velthouse (1990) define empowerment as the increased intrinsic motivation of employees to take ownership of their work. Empowered employees are more likely to take initiative in identifying lessons learned and applying them to improve future projects.

Organizational culture significantly impacts the effectiveness of lessons learned practices. A culture that values continuous learning, openness, and collaboration creates an environment where lessons learned can be effectively captured, shared, and applied. By fostering a culture that supports these key aspects, organizations can enhance their ability to learn from past experiences and improve future project performance. This chapter has highlighted the profound influence of organizational culture on lessons learned and provided evidence from both literature and my dissertation to support these insights.

Understanding Cognitive Moderators

Cognitive moderators are factors that influence the degree to which cognitive biases impact decision-making. These moderators can either amplify or mitigate the effects of cognitive biases, and they are often under the control of the organization. Unlike biases, which are the symptoms, cognitive moderators can be the underlying causes affecting the quality of decisions. Incorporating strategies to manage these moderators can significantly improve decision- making and foster a culture of continuous learning.

Psychological Safety

Psychological safety refers to an environment where individuals feel safe taking interpersonal risks, such as admitting mistakes or asking for help, without fear of negative consequences. Edmondson (1999) found that teams with high psychological safety are more likely to engage in learning behaviors, such as discussing errors and seeking feedback, which are crucial for effective lessons learned practices.

Cognitive Load

Cognitive load theory suggests that the human brain has limited capacity for processing information. When cognitive load is high, decision-making quality can decrease (Sweller, 1988). Organizations can reduce cognitive load by streamlining processes, reducing unnecessary complexity, and providing adequate resources and support to employees.

Decision Fatigue

Decision fatigue occurs when the quality of decisions deteriorates after an extended period of decision-making. Baumeister et al. (1998) demonstrated that individuals with decision fatigue are more likely to make impulsive or suboptimal choices. Organizations can mitigate decision fatigue by implementing decision-making protocols that include breaks and delegation strategies.

Noise

Noise, as described by Kahneman et al. (2022), refers to the variability in judgments that should be identical. Noise can be reduced by standardizing decision-making processes and using checklists and decision aids. Consistent training and calibration sessions can also help minimize noise in organizational decisions.

Inertia

Inertia is the resistance to change and the tendency to stick with existing practices. Overcoming inertia requires strong leadership and a culture that encourages experimentation and adaptation. Providing clear rationales for change and involving employees in the change process can help mitigate inertia (Hannon & Freeman, 1984).

Time Pressure

Time pressure can lead to rushed decisions and increased reliance on heuristics, which can amplify cognitive biases (Ordóñez & Benson, 1997). Organizations can manage time pressure by setting realistic deadlines, prioritizing tasks effectively, and ensuring that employees have sufficient time to make considered decisions.

Social Pressure

Social pressure influences individuals to conform to group norms or expectations, which can stifle innovation and critical thinking. Asch (1956) demonstrated how social pressure can lead to conformity. Creating a culture that values diverse perspectives and encourages independent thinking can help reduce the negative impact of social pressure.

Leadership's Role in Managing Cognitive Moderators

Leadership plays a crucial role in managing cognitive moderators. By fostering an environment of psychological safety, reducing cognitive load, managing decision fatigue, and addressing other moderators, leaders can enhance decision-making quality and promote a culture of continuous improvement. Implementing structured decision-making processes and providing training on cognitive biases and moderators can further support these efforts (Yukl, 2012).

CASE STUDY: GOOGLE

Google is renowned for its culture of innovation and continuous improvement. One of the key elements of Google's success is its strong emphasis on learning from both successes and failures. The company's post-mortem process for projects ensures that lessons learned are captured and shared across teams, fostering a culture of transparency and continuous learning (Schmidt & Rosenberg, 2014).

Google's Post-Mortem Process

Google's post-mortem process involves a systematic review of projects to identify what went well and what could be improved. This process is designed to be transparent, with a focus on constructive feedback and learning rather than assigning blame. According to Collier et al. (1996), a structured post- mortem review includes specific activities, roles, and artifacts that contribute to organizational learning. These reviews help in documenting risks and planning for future projects by incorporating lessons learned into risk management strategies.

Methodology and Benefits

The methodology for conducting post-mortems at Google is grounded in continuous process improvement. Tiedeman (1990) describes how post-mortems can be systematically conducted to review both the product quality and the associated processes. By doing so, organizations can gain insights into what worked well and identify areas for improvement. This methodology has proven effective in generating actionable lessons that lead to improved project outcomes and innovation.

Learning from Experience

Learning from both successes and failures is crucial for fostering innovation. Stålhane et al. (2003) emphasize that post-mortem analyses (PMAs) are valuable for harvesting experience from completed projects. These analyses can be part of a larger knowledge management program, helping organizations document their knowledge, identify improvement actions, and systematically learn from their projects.

Google's rigorous post-mortem process and emphasis on continuous learning from both successes and failures have significantly contributed to its culture of innovation and project success. This approach ensures that valuable lessons are systematically captured, shared, and applied to future projects.

CASE STUDY: TOYOTA

Toyota's commitment to continuous improvement, known as Kaizen, is deeply embedded in its organizational culture. The practice of regularly reviewing and learning from past projects has been integral to Toyota's ability to innovate and improve its manufacturing processes. This culture of continuous improvement has contributed significantly to Toyota's success as a global leader in the automotive industry (Liker, 2004).

Kaizen in Practice

Kaizen, which means "good change" in Japanese, involves making small, incremental improvements in processes to enhance efficiency and eliminate waste. At Toyota, Kaizen is not just a set of practices but a core part of the organizational culture. It involves everyone, from top management to frontline workers, continuously seeking ways to improve their work processes.

Shumpei Iwao (2018) observed that Kaizen activities at Toyota are characterized by a series of innovations with various scales, including small changes in product design and significant organizational activities in production design. These activities often involve product/process design engineers and shop floor engineers working together, emphasizing the collaborative nature of Kaizen at Toyota.

Organizational and Knowledge Management

The success of Kaizen at Toyota is also attributed to its robust organizational and knowledge management frameworks. Rémy Magnier-Watanabe (2011) highlighted that Toyota's organizational design and the alignment of Kaizen with the overall corporate strategy are critical for its effective implementation. This alignment ensures that Kaizen activities are not isolated efforts but are integrated into the company's broader goals and objectives.

Impact on Performance

Kaizen has significantly improved Toyota's operational performance. H. Abdulmouti (2015) discussed how implementing Kaizen principles at Toyota's Port Installed Options Center in Saudi Arabia led to a 26.9% reduction in manpower and a 13% increase in annual output. This improvement in efficiency and productivity underscores the effectiveness of Kaizen in optimizing manufacturing processes.

Toyota's commitment to continuous improvement through Kaizen has been instrumental in its success. The integration of Kaizen into every aspect of its operations ensures ongoing enhancements in efficiency, quality, and innovation. This culture of continuous improvement not only drives Toyota's operational success but also sets a benchmark for other organizations aiming to adopt similar practices.

CASE STUDY: IBM

IBM's cultural transformation focused on fostering a culture of openness and knowledge sharing. By implementing a comprehensive lessons learned process and encouraging collaboration across teams, IBM enhanced its project management practices and drove innovation. The company's leadership played a crucial role in promoting this cultural shift (Gerstner, 2003).

Knowledge Sharing and Organizational Culture

IBM's transformation involved embedding knowledge sharing into the core of its organizational culture. According to Huang (1997), IBM's approach to Intellectual Capital Management (ICM) aimed to institutionalize knowledge management across its global services and industries. This included creating an infrastructure and processes for knowledge creation, sharing, and utilization, which helped IBM adapt to changing conditions and continuously improve its practices.

Implementation of Lessons Learned Processes

IBM's implementation of lessons learned processes was comprehensive, involving both formal and informal practices. A study by Mueller (2015) indicated that while formal mechanisms for knowledge sharing are essential, informal practices developed by employees and project leaders also play a significant role in effective knowledge transfer. These practices foster a collaborative culture that enhances project management outcomes.

Barriers and Enablers of Knowledge Sharing

Despite the benefits, IBM faced challenges in fostering a culture of knowledge sharing. Eskerod and Skriver (2007) identified several organizational cultural barriers that can limit knowledge transfer, such as subcultures within the organization and reluctance to share knowledge due to competitive pressures. Overcoming these barriers required targeted strategies to align organizational culture with knowledge management initiatives.

Impact on Innovation and Project Management

The transformation at IBM had a profound impact on its project management and innovation capabilities. Almeida and Soares (2014) emphasized that effective knowledge sharing in project-based organizations (PBOs) like IBM leads to improved organizational learning and project performance. They highlighted that both codified and personalized knowledge-sharing strategies are crucial for maximizing the benefits of lessons learned processes.

IBM's cultural transformation towards openness and knowledge sharing, driven by its comprehensive lessons learned processes and leadership support, has significantly enhanced its project management practices and innovation capabilities. By overcoming cultural barriers and fostering a collaborative environment, IBM has set a benchmark for effective knowledge management in large organizations.

In a quantitative correlational study by Cunio (2024), significant correlations were found between organizational culture and the successful implementation of lessons learned practices. Key findings included:

1. **Positive Correlation with Revenue Growth:** Organizations that foster a culture of continuous learning and knowledge sharing showed higher revenue growth compared to those that did not prioritize these cultural elements. By encouraging continuous learning and open exchange of knowledge, these organizations could adapt more effectively to changes and innovations, leading to improved financial performance. This positive correlation underscores the strategic value of cultivating a learning- oriented culture.

2. **Enhanced Project Outcomes:** Teams operating within a supportive culture that values lessons learned reported improved project outcomes, including better adherence to timelines, budgets, and quality standards. Such a culture promotes thorough post-project reviews and encourages the application of insights gained from past projects to current and future projects. This practice leads to more efficient project management and higher-quality deliverables.

3. **Increased Employee Engagement:** A culture that empowers employees to actively participate in the lessons learned process led to higher levels of employee engagement and satisfaction. When employees feel their contributions are valued and that they can influence organizational practices, their engagement and commitment to the organization increase. This heightened engagement contributes to overall project success and organizational resilience.

Creating a culture that values lessons learned requires deliberate effort and strategic initiatives. Here are some strategies to foster a learning culture:

1. **Leadership Commitment:** Leaders must demonstrate a commitment to learning and improvement by actively participating in the lessons learned process and encouraging their teams to do the same (Kotter, 1996).

   Alex's Experience: Alex worked with senior leadership to promote the importance of lessons learned. By presenting data on the benefits of lessons learned and sharing success stories, Alex gained leadership buy-in, which helped foster a culture that values continuous improvement.

2. **Incentivize Knowledge Sharing:** Recognize and reward employees who actively contribute to the lessons learned process. Incentives can include formal recognition, career advancement opportunities, and performance bonuses (Thomas & Velthouse, 1990).

   Alex's Experience: Alex introduced a recognition program where team members who contributed valuable lessons were acknowledged in team meetings and company newsletters. This incentivized participation and highlighted the importance of sharing knowledge.

3. **Provide Training and Resources:** Offer training programs and resources to help employees understand the importance of lessons learned and how to effectively capture and apply them (Senge, 2006).

Alex's Experience: Alex organized training sessions to educate team members on the principles of lessons learned and the PILL Framework. Providing resources such as templates and guides made it easier for team members to participate in the process.

4. **Create Safe Spaces for Learning:** Foster an environment where employees feel safe to share their experiences, including failures, without fear of blame or retribution. This openness is crucial for capturing valuable lessons (Edmondson, 1999).

   Alex's Experience: Alex encouraged open discussions about failures and successes in team meetings. By promoting a no-blame culture, team members felt more comfortable sharing their experiences, leading to more honest and insightful lessons learned.

5. **Leverage Technology:** Use technology platforms to facilitate the capture, storage, and dissemination of lessons learned. Collaborative tools and knowledge management systems can enhance accessibility and usability (Nonaka & Takeuchi, 1995).

   Alex's Experience: Alex implemented a knowledge management system that allowed team members to document and share lessons learned in real-time. This platform made it easier to store and retrieve lessons, ensuring that valuable insights were not lost.

6. **Regularly Review and Apply Lessons:** Ensure that lessons learned are regularly reviewed and integrated into project planning and execution. This continuous application reinforces the value of lessons learned and embeds them into the organizational culture (Schmidt & Rosenberg, 2014).

   Alex's Experience: Alex scheduled regular reviews of lessons learned during project planning sessions. By integrating these insights into new projects, Alex ensured that the team continuously improved and avoided repeating past mistakes.

7. **Encourage Cross-Functional Collaboration:** Promote collaboration across different teams and departments to share lessons learned and apply them to a broader range of projects. This cross-functional approach can lead to more innovative solutions and improvements (Gerstner, 2003).

Alex's Experience: **Alex** facilitated cross-functional workshops where different teams shared their lessons learned. This collaboration led to the discovery of new insights and best practices that were applied across multiple projects, enhancing overall project success.

By implementing these strategies, organizations can create a culture that values lessons learned, driving continuous improvement, and leading to better project outcomes and overall organizational success.

Conclusion

The exploration of organizational culture's role in lessons learned practices underscores its critical importance in achieving sustained project management success. Organizational culture shapes how team members perceive, value, and engage with lessons learned, significantly influencing the effectiveness of these practices. This chapter has highlighted the profound impact that a supportive and learning-oriented culture can have on the continuous improvement of project outcomes.

Alex's journey within his organization vividly illustrates the challenges and triumphs associated with fostering a culture that values lessons learned. By addressing resistance to change, promoting knowledge sharing, and securing leadership support, Alex was able to embed lessons learned practices into the organizational fabric. This cultural shift not only improved project performance but also cultivated an environment of openness and innovation.

Impact of Organizational Culture on Lessons Learned

◊ **Positive Correlation with Revenue Growth:** Organizations that foster a culture of continuous learning and knowledge sharing often see higher revenue growth. This correlation underscores the financial benefits of investing in a supportive organizational culture.

◊ **Enhanced Project Outcomes:** Teams operating within a culture that values lessons learned consistently report better adherence to timelines, budgets, and quality standards. This alignment leads to more successful project outcomes.

◊ **Increased Employee Engagement:** Empowering employees to actively participate in lessons learned processes leads to higher levels of engagement and satisfaction. This empowerment drives motivation and contributes to a positive organizational atmosphere.

Strategies for Fostering a Learning Culture

◊ **Leadership Commitment:** Leaders play a pivotal role in promoting and sustaining a learning culture. By actively participating in lessons learned processes and setting a positive example, leaders can encourage widespread adoption.

◊ **Incentivizing Knowledge Sharing:** Recognizing and rewarding employees who contribute to lessons learned fosters a culture of openness and collaboration. Incentives can range from formal recognition to performance bonuses.

◊ **Providing Training and Resources:** Offering regular training and resources ensures that team members understand the importance of lessons learned and are equipped to capture and apply them effectively.

◊ **Creating Safe Spaces for Learning:** Promoting psychological safety encourages team members to share their experiences without fear of retribution. This openness is crucial for capturing honest and valuable insights.

◊ **Leveraging Technology:** Using technology platforms to facilitate the capture, storage, and dissemination of lessons learned enhances accessibility and usability. Collaborative tools can streamline the process and ensure that valuable insights are not lost.

◊ **Regularly Reviewing and Applying Lessons:** Systematic reviews and integration of lessons learned into project planning and execution reinforce the value of continuous improvement.

◊ **Encouraging Cross-Functional Collaboration:** Promoting collaboration across different teams and departments can lead to the discovery of innovative solutions and best practices.

Alex's efforts to foster a learning culture within his organization demonstrate the transformative potential of these strategies. By creating an environment where team members feel valued and empowered, Alex was able to drive significant improvements in project performance and overall organizational success.

Moving Forward

As we move forward, the next chapter will explore the integration of behavioral science principles into lessons learned practices. Understanding how cognitive biases and social dynamics influence decision-making can significantly enhance the effectiveness of these practices. By applying behavioral science insights, project managers can develop strategies to mitigate biases and foster a culture of continuous improvement.

The importance of organizational culture in lessons learned practices cannot be overstated. A supportive, learning-oriented culture is essential for effectively capturing, sharing, and applying valuable insights. By implementing the strategies discussed in this chapter, project managers can cultivate a culture that not only values lessons learned but also drives continuous improvement and innovation. Alex's journey exemplifies how a strong organizational culture can transform lessons learned from a theoretical concept into a practical, impactful practice. As you continue exploring the subsequent chapters, you will gain deeper insights and tools to further enhance your lessons learned practices, ensuring your organization achieves sustainable success through continuous learning and adaptation.

Chapter Insights

_____

_____

_____

_____

_____

_____

_____

_____

_____

_____

_____

_____

_____

_____

_____

_____

_____

CHAPTER 6

Behavioral Science and Lessons Learned

Introduction to Behavioral Science

Behavioral science explores how human behavior impacts decision-making, often uncovering insights that are not immediately apparent. In project management, understanding behavioral science is essential for implementing effective lessons learned practices. Cognitive biases, social dynamics, and individual behaviors can all influence how lessons are captured, shared, and applied. Recognizing these influences enables project managers to design better strategies for continuous improvement and effective knowledge management.

Understanding Cognitive Biases

Cognitive biases are systematic patterns of deviation from norm or rationality in judgment that can significantly impact project management and the effectiveness of lessons learned practices. Key cognitive biases relevant to project management include:

Optimism Bias: The tendency to overestimate the likelihood of positive outcomes and underestimate the likelihood of negative ones. This bias can lead project teams to set unrealistic timelines and budgets, expecting everything to proceed smoothly without accounting for potential setbacks (Tversky & Kahneman, 1974).

Confirmation Bias: The tendency to seek out, interpret, and remember information that confirms preexisting beliefs. This bias can cause project managers to overlook critical feedback and warnings, leading to flawed decision-making and ignored risks (Nickerson, 1998).

Status Quo Bias: The preference for the current state of affairs and resistance to change. This bias can hinder innovation and adaptability, as team members may prefer to stick with familiar methods and processes, even if they are suboptimal (Samuelson & Zeckhauser, 1988).

Table 6.1: Strategies to Mitigate Cognitive Biases

Cognitive Bias	Mitigation Strategy
Optimism Bias	Conservative estimates, contingency planning
Confirmation Bias	Diverse perspectives, data validation
Status Quo Bias	Encouraging innovation, regular reviews

Heuristics in Decision-Making

Heuristics are mental shortcuts people use to make decisions quickly and efficiently. While they can be useful, heuristics often lead to cognitive biases that impact the lessons learned process. For example:

◊ **Availability Heuristic:** Overestimating the importance of information that is readily available or recent. This can lead to overemphasizing recent project issues while neglecting older but equally important problems (Ramirez & De Baets, 2021).

◊ **Anchoring Effect:** Relying too heavily on the first piece of information encountered when making decisions. This can skew project estimates and planning if the initial information is inaccurate (Ramirez & De Baets, 2021).

Understanding these heuristics helps identify potential biases in the lessons learned process and take steps to mitigate their impact.

Impact of Biases on Project Management

Cognitive biases can affect various aspects of project management, including risk assessment, decision-making, and team dynamics. For example, optimism bias may lead to underestimating project risks, resulting in insufficient contingency planning. Confirmation bias can result in disregarding critical feedback that contradicts existing plans, while status quo bias may prevent teams from adopting new and more efficient practices. Understanding and mitigating these biases is essential for improving the accuracy and effectiveness of lessons learned practices.

Alex's Experience with Cognitive Biases

Alex noticed that their team often fell prey to optimism bias, consistently underestimating the time required to complete tasks. Recognizing this bias, Alex introduced more conservative time estimates and contingency planning, which improved project timelines. By adjusting the team's approach to planning and risk management, Alex was able to create a more realistic and reliable project schedule.

Understanding the impact of cognitive biases, Alex implemented regular reflection sessions where team members could discuss their assumptions and challenge each other's perspectives. This practice helped mitigate the effects of optimism and confirmation biases.

Mitigating Cognitive Biases

To counteract cognitive biases, project managers can implement several strategies:

1. **Data-Driven Decision-Making:** Using empirical data and statistical analysis to guide decisions can help mitigate biases. By relying on objective data rather than subjective judgments, project managers can make more accurate and informed decisions (Ramirez & De Baets, 2021).

2. **Diverse Perspectives:** Encouraging input from a diverse group of stakeholders can reduce the impact of confirmation bias. Diverse teams bring different viewpoints and experiences, which can help challenge assumptions and uncover blind spots (Turner & Müller, 2005).

3. **Structured Frameworks:** Adopting structured decision-making frameworks provides a systematic approach to evaluating options and risks. These frameworks help ensure that all relevant factors are considered and that decisions are based on thorough analysis (Kerzner, 2022).

Behavioral Analysis in Project Management

Behavioral analysis involves examining the behaviors of individuals and teams to identify patterns that may impact project outcomes. Key areas of focus include:

1. **Team Dynamics:** Understanding how team interactions and relationships affect performance. Effective team dynamics are crucial for collaboration and productivity. Behavioral analysis can help identify issues such as communication breakdowns or conflict and develop strategies to improve team cohesion.

2. **Motivational Factors:** Identifying what motivates team members and how to leverage these motivations to enhance performance. Understanding individual and collective motivations can help project managers design incentive structures and work environments that boost morale and productivity.

3. **Communication Patterns:** Analyzing how information is shared within the team and how communication can be improved. Effective communication is essential for successful project management. By

studying communication patterns, project managers can identify bottlenecks and barriers to information flow and implement practices to ensure clear, timely, and accurate communication (Schein, 2010).

CASE STUDY: BEHAVIORAL INSIGHTS IN PROJECT MANAGEMENT

A software development company implemented behavioral analysis to improve project outcomes. By analyzing team dynamics, they identified communication breakdowns as a source of delays. The company introduced regular team-building activities and communication training, which led to improved collaboration and project success (Edmondson, 1999).

Role of Team Dynamics

Effective team dynamics are crucial for the success of agile project management in software development. A systematic literature review by Jallow et al. (2023) found that factors such as effective communication, collaboration, skills, and knowledge significantly contribute to the success of agile projects. Improving team dynamics directly impacts project performance by enhancing collaboration and efficiency (Jallow et al., 2023).

Impact of Communication and Emotional Capability

Effective communication within teams is essential for managing project risks and ensuring timely project delivery. Akgün et al. (2011) found that emotional capability, including dynamics of encouragement, experiencing, and reconciliation, plays a significant role in enhancing team performance and project success. Promoting emotional capability through team autonomy and collaboration leads to better market success for software products (Akgün et al., 2011).

Enhancing Collaboration through Team-Building Activities

Introducing regular team-building activities and communication training can significantly improve team collaboration. Research indicates that structured communication patterns and effective use of communication channels are crucial for successful project management (Kerzner, 2022). Fostering an environment where team members understand the importance of clear and consistent communication enhances team coordination and performance.

Implementing behavioral insights in project management, particularly through analyzing team dynamics and improving communication, can lead to significant improvements in project outcomes. Regular team-building activities and communication training are effective strategies for enhancing collaboration and achieving project success.

ALEX'S EXPERIENCE WITH BEHAVIORAL ANALYSIS

Alex used behavioral analysis to identify that some team members were hesitant to share their ideas due to a perceived lack of psychological safety. By fostering an inclusive and supportive environment, Alex encouraged more open communication, which led to better problem-solving and innovation.

1. **NASA's Mars Climate Orbiter:** The failure of the Mars Climate Orbiter in 1999 was partly attributed to cognitive biases such as overconfidence and groupthink. The mission team did not thoroughly check calculations and assumptions, leading to a critical error where one team used metric units while another used imperial units. This oversight resulted in the spacecraft entering the Martian atmosphere at the wrong trajectory and disintegrating. The incident highlights the importance of rigorous validation and verification processes to counteract cognitive biases (NASA, 1999).

2. **The Challenger Disaster:** The Challenger disaster in 1986 was significantly influenced by groupthink and pressure to conform. Engineers expressed concerns about the O-rings' performance in the cold temperatures expected on the launch day, but their warnings were downplayed or ignored due to organizational pressures to proceed with the launch. This tragic event underscores the dangers of groupthink, where the desire for consensus overrides the evaluation of alternative viewpoints and critical information (Vaughan, 2016).

Practical Applications of Behavioral Science

To effectively apply behavioral science principles in lessons learned practices, project managers can implement the following strategies:

1. **Foster Psychological Safety:** Creating an environment where team members feel safe to express their thoughts and concerns without fear of retribution is crucial for effective lessons learned practices. Psychological safety encourages open communication, honesty, and the

sharing both successes and failures. Techniques to foster psychological safety include encouraging respectful dialogue, actively listening to team members, and acknowledging and learning from mistakes rather than assigning blame (Edmondson, 1999).

2. **Implement Bias Awareness Training:** Educating team members about common cognitive biases and how to recognize them is essential for mitigating their impact on project management. Bias awareness training helps individuals understand how biases like optimism bias, confirmation bias, and status quo bias can affect their judgment and decision-making processes. This awareness leads to more balanced and objective decision-making, enhancing the effectiveness of lessons learned practices (Tversky & Kahneman, 1974).

3. **Use Reflective Practices:** Encouraging regular reflection on individual and team behaviors is a powerful way to identify areas for improvement and promote continuous learning. Reflective practices involve structured activities such as after-action reviews, debriefing sessions, and journaling. By reflecting on their experiences, team members can gain deeper insights into their behaviors and decisions, leading to more informed and effective lessons learned (Schein, 2010).

Additional Strategies for Applying Behavioral Science

4. **Encourage Diverse Perspectives:** Actively seeking out and valuing diverse perspectives within the team can help counteract cognitive biases and lead to more robust decision-making. Diversity in backgrounds, experiences, and viewpoints can challenge groupthink and provide a more comprehensive understanding of project challenges and opportunities.

5. **Leverage Data and Analytics:** Using data and analytics to inform lessons learned practices can help project managers make more evidence- based

decisions. By systematically collecting and analyzing project data, teams can identify patterns, trends, and root causes of issues. Data-driven insights can provide an objective basis for understanding what worked and what didn't, reducing the influence of subjective biases.

6. **Promote a Growth Mindset:** Cultivating a growth mindset within the team can enhance the willingness to learn from mistakes and embrace challenges. A growth mindset, as described by Carol Dweck, involves believing that abilities and intelligence can be developed through effort and learning. This mindset fosters resilience and a proactive approach to problem-solving, which are critical for effective lessons learned practices.

Applying behavioral science principles to lessons learned practices can significantly enhance their effectiveness and impact. By fostering psychological safety, implementing bias awareness training, encouraging reflective practices, valuing diverse perspectives, leveraging data, and promoting a growth mindset, project managers can create an environment that supports continuous learning and improvement. These strategies help ensure that lessons learned are not only captured but also meaningfully applied to drive better project outcomes and organizational success.

ALEX'S EXPERIENCE WITH REFLECTIVE PRACTICES

Alex implemented regular reflection sessions where team members could discuss their assumptions and challenge each other's perspectives. This practice helped mitigate the effects of optimism and confirmation biases, leading to more accurate project planning and execution.

By understanding and addressing heuristics and cognitive biases, project managers can significantly enhance the effectiveness of their lessons learned practices. Integrating behavioral science insights into project management not only improves decision-making but also fosters a culture of continuous improvement and innovation. Alex's journey serves as a practical example of how these principles can be applied to achieve better project outcomes and create a more resilient and adaptive team.

Conclusion

Integrating behavioral science into lessons learned practices provides a nuanced understanding of how human behavior impacts project management. Cognitive biases, social dynamics, and individual behaviors significantly influence the effectiveness of lessons learned processes. By recognizing and addressing these factors, project managers can create a more robust and effective approach to continuous improvement.

Alex's journey highlights the critical role of behavioral science in enhancing lessons learned practices. By understanding cognitive biases such as optimism bias, confirmation bias, and status quo bias, Alex implemented strategies that mitigated their impact on project decision-making. This approach not only improved project outcomes but also fostered a culture of reflection and openness within the team.

Understanding Cognitive Biases

◊ **Optimism Bias:** The tendency to overestimate the likelihood of positive outcomes and underestimate potential risks can lead to unrealistic project plans and expectations. By acknowledging this bias, Alex implemented more conservative time estimates and contingency plans, resulting in more realistic project timelines.

◊ **Confirmation Bias:** The tendency to search for, interpret, and remember information that confirms preconceptions can hinder objective decision-making. Alex encouraged diverse perspectives and data validation processes to counteract this bias, leading to more balanced and informed decisions.

◊ **Status Quo Bias:** The preference for maintaining the current state of affairs can resist necessary changes. Alex fostered a culture of innovation and regular reviews, encouraging the team to challenge the status quo and embrace continuous improvement.

Mitigating Cognitive Biases

◊ **Data-Driven Decision Making:** Using empirical data and statistical analysis helps mitigate biases by grounding decisions in factual evidence. Alex's reliance on data-driven insights ensured that project decisions were objective and reliable.

◊ **Diverse Perspectives:** Encouraging input from a diverse group of stakeholders helps reduce the impact of confirmation bias. Alex's inclusive approach to decision-making ensured that multiple viewpoints were considered, leading to more comprehensive solutions.

◊ **Structured Frameworks:** Adopting structured decision-making frameworks provides a systematic approach to evaluating options and risks. Alex's use of the PILL Framework ensured that lessons learned were systematically captured, analyzed, and applied.

Practical Applications of Behavioral Science

◊ **Foster Psychological Safety:** Creating an environment where team members feel safe to express their thoughts and concerns without fear of retribution is crucial. Alex promoted psychological safety by encouraging open discussions about successes and failures during team meetings.

◊ **Implement Bias Awareness Training:** Educating team members about common cognitive biases and how to recognize them can significantly improve decision-making processes. Alex organized regular training sessions to raise awareness and mitigate the impact of biases.

◊ **Use Reflective Practices:** Regular reflection on individual and team behaviors helps identify areas for improvement. Alex implemented reflective practices, such as after-action reviews and retrospectives, to continuously refine project processes.

 **ALEX'S EXPERIENCE WITH BEHAVIORAL SCIENCE**

Alex's application of behavioral science principles provided valuable insights into the human factors affecting project management. By addressing cognitive biases and fostering a culture of openness, Alex was able to enhance the team's ability to capture and apply lessons learned effectively. This holistic approach to lessons learned practices not only improved project outcomes but also contributed to the overall growth and development of the team.

Moving Forward

As we move forward, the next chapter will explore practical applications and tools for implementing lessons learned practices. It will provide templates, software solutions, and methodologies that project managers can use to enhance their lessons learned processes. By leveraging these tools, you can systematically capture, analyze, and apply lessons learned to drive continuous improvement in your projects.

Integrating behavioral science into lessons learned practices offers a powerful approach to enhancing project management capabilities. By understanding and addressing cognitive biases and social dynamics, project managers can create a more effective and reflective approach to continuous improvement. Alex's journey serves as a compelling example of how behavioral science can transform lessons learned from a theoretical concept into a practical, impactful practice. As you continue to explore the subsequent chapters, you will gain deeper insights and tools to further enhance your lessons learned practices, ensuring that your organization can achieve sustainable success through continuous learning and adaptation.

Chapter Insights

_____

_____

_____

_____

_____

_____

_____

_____

_____

_____

_____

_____

_____

_____

_____

_____

_____

CHAPTER 7

Practical Applications and Tools

Introduction to Practical Applications and Tools

Implementing lessons learned practices effectively requires practical tools and applications that can be seamlessly integrated into project management processes. This chapter explores various templates, software solutions, and methodologies that project managers, like Alex, can use to enhance their lessons learned practices. By leveraging these tools, project managers can systematically capture, analyze, and apply lessons learned to improve project outcomes and foster a culture of continuous improvement.

Templates for Capturing Lessons Learned

Templates provide a structured format for capturing and documenting lessons learned. They ensure consistency and completeness in the information recorded, making it easier to analyze and share insights. Key elements typically included in lessons learned templates are:

1. **Project Information:** Basic details about the project, including name, duration, team members, and objectives.

2. **Lesson Description:** A clear and concise description of what was learned, including both successes and challenges.

3. **Root Cause Analysis:** An examination of the underlying reasons for the outcomes observed, identifying what led to the success or issue.

4. **Recommendations:** Practical advice and strategies for future projects based on the lesson learned.

5. **Action Items:** Specific steps to be taken to apply the lesson learned to future projects.

By using standardized templates, project managers can ensure that all relevant information is captured systematically and comprehensively.

Software Solutions for Lessons Learned

Technology plays a crucial role in facilitating lessons learned practices. Various software solutions can help project managers capture, store, and disseminate lessons learned more effectively. Some popular software tools include:

1. Knowledge Management Systems (KMS)

◊ **Examples:** SharePoint, Confluence

◊ **Functionality:** These platforms provide centralized repositories for storing lessons learned, making them easily accessible to all team members. They support document management, collaboration, and search capabilities, ensuring that valuable insights are not lost and can be retrieved when needed.

2. Project Management Software

◊ **Examples:** Asana, Trello, Jira

◊ **Functionality:** These tools integrate lessons learned processes into project workflows. They allow project managers to document lessons learned as tasks or comments within the project management system, ensuring that insights are captured in real-time and linked to specific project activities.

3. Collaborative Platforms

◊ **Examples:** Slack, Microsoft Teams

◊ **Functionality:** Collaborative tools facilitate communication and knowledge sharing among team members. They provide channels or spaces dedicated to lessons learned, enabling real-time discussions and quick dissemination of insights.

4. Data Analytics Tools

◊ **Examples:** Tableau, Power BI

◊ **Functionality:** These tools help project managers analyze lessons learned data to identify trends and patterns. They offer visualization capabilities that make it easier to interpret complex data and derive actionable insights.

Methodologies for Applying Lessons Learned

Integrating lessons learned into project management processes requires adopting methodologies that promote continuous improvement. Some effective methodologies include:

1. After-Action Reviews (AARs)

◊ **Description:** AARs are structured debriefing sessions conducted after project phases or significant events. They involve the project team discussing what happened, why it happened, and how it can be improved in the future.

◊ **Benefits:** AARs provide immediate feedback and facilitate the identification of lessons learned while the experiences are still fresh in team members' minds.

2. Retrospectives

◊ **Description:** Commonly used in Agile project management, retrospectives are regular meetings where the project team reflects on their recent work and identifies areas for improvement.

◊ **Benefits:** Retrospectives encourage continuous learning and adaptation, helping teams make incremental improvements throughout the project lifecycle.

3. Root Cause Analysis (RCA)

◊ **Description:** RCA is a problem-solving method used to identify the underlying causes of issues or successes. Techniques such as the "5 Whys" and fishbone diagrams are commonly used in RCA.

◊ **Benefits:** RCA helps project managers understand the root causes of outcomes and develop targeted strategies to address them.

◊ **Note:** RCAs should be completed during Step 3: Analyzing for the PILL Framework. This is crucial to understanding if the captured information is an actual lesson learned. The RCA can also reveal that the initial information captured is not a lesson learned, but rather the root cause of an observation.

4. Knowledge Sharing Sessions

◊ **Description:** Regularly scheduled meetings or workshops where team members share their experiences and lessons learned from various projects.

◊ **Benefits:** These sessions foster a culture of knowledge sharing and collaboration, ensuring that valuable insights are disseminated across the organization.

ALEX'S IMPLEMENTATION OF TOOLS AND METHODOLOGIES

Alex successfully integrated these tools and methodologies into his project management practices:

◊ **Using Templates:** Alex standardized the documentation process for lessons learned by implementing templates that captured all essential information. This ensured consistency and made it easier to analyze and apply lessons across projects.

◊ **Leveraging Software:** Alex adopted a knowledge management system to store and share lessons learned. He also used project management software to integrate lessons learned into the workflow, allowing real-time documentation and tracking.

◊ **Conducting AARs and Retrospectives:** Alex regularly conducted AARs and retrospectives, creating a habit of continuous reflection and improvement within the team.

◊ **Implementing RCA:** When issues arose, Alex used RCAs to understand the underlying factors and develop effective solutions. This approach helped prevent the recurrence of the same problems in future projects.

◊ **Facilitating Knowledge Sharing Sessions:** Alex organized monthly knowledge-sharing sessions where team members could discuss their experiences and learn from each other. These sessions promoted a culture of learning and collaboration.

Practical applications and tools are essential for effectively implementing lessons learned practices in project management. By leveraging templates, software solutions, and methodologies, project managers like Alex can systematically capture, analyze, and apply lessons learned to enhance project outcomes and foster a culture of continuous improvement.

CASE STUDY: SOFTWARE IMPLEMENTATION

A global IT firm implemented a knowledge management system to enhance its lessons learned process. By centralizing lessons learned documentation and making it easily accessible, the firm improved its ability to apply lessons across multiple projects, leading to a 20% increase in project success rates (Williams, 2008).

ALEX'S EXPERIENCE WITH SOFTWARE SOLUTIONS

Alex implemented a knowledge management system that allowed team members to document and share lessons learned in real-time. This platform also provided analytical tools to identify trends and insights from the captured data, enhancing the overall lessons learned process.

Alex found that using a knowledge management system not only streamlined the documentation process but also made it easier for the team to access and apply past lessons, leading to continuous improvement.

Workshops and Training Modules

Regular workshops and training sessions are essential for educating team members about the importance of lessons learned and how to effectively capture and apply them. These sessions not only build skills but also foster a culture of continuous improvement and knowledge sharing. A well-structured training program ensures that all team members understand their roles in the lessons learned process and are equipped with the necessary tools and techniques to contribute effectively.

Key Components of a Successful Training Program

1. Introduction to Lessons Learned: Overview of the Concepts and Benefits

Objective: To provide a foundational understanding of lessons learned practices and their significance in project management.

Content:

◊ Definition and purpose of lessons learned.

◊ Historical context and evolution of lessons learned in project management.

◊ Key benefits, including risk mitigation, continuous improvement, and enhanced organizational learning.

◊ Real-life examples and case studies illustrating successful lessons learned practices.

Outcome: Participants will appreciate the value of lessons learned and recognize their role in fostering a learning-oriented culture.

2. Capturing Lessons Learned: Techniques and Best Practices

Objective: To teach effective methods for identifying and documenting lessons learned throughout the project lifecycle.

Content:

◊ Techniques for capturing lessons learned during project execution, such as after-action reviews and reflective practices.

◊ Best practice for documenting lessons in a structured and consistent manner.

◊ Tips for encouraging team participation and openness in sharing experiences.

◊ Tools and templates for standardizing the documentation process.

Outcome: Participants will be able to systematically capture valuable insights and experiences from their projects.

3. Analyzing and Prioritizing Lessons: Methods for Evaluating and Prioritizing Lessons

Objective: To develop skills for analyzing captured lessons and determining their relevance and priority.

Content:

◊ Methods for categorizing and organizing lessons learned.

◊ Criteria for evaluating the impact and applicability of lessons.

◊ Techniques for prioritizing lessons based on their potential to improve future project outcomes.

◊ Use of data analytics and root cause analysis to uncover underlying issues and trends.

Outcome: Participants will be able to critically evaluate lessons learned and prioritize them for implementation.

4. Implementing Lessons Learned: Strategies for Applying Lessons to Future Projects

Objective: To provide strategies for effectively applying lessons learned to enhance future project performance.

Content:

◊ Steps for integrating lessons learned into project planning and execution phases.

◊ Strategies for ensuring lessons learned are communicated and accessible to all relevant stakeholders.

◊ Techniques for monitoring the implementation of lessons learned and measuring their impact.

◊ Overcoming common challenges in applying lessons learned, such as resistance to change and knowledge silos.

Outcome: Participants will be equipped with practical strategies to implement lessons learned in their projects, leading to continuous improvement.

5. Using Technology: Training on the Specific Tools and Software Used by the Organization

Objective: To familiarize team members with the technological tools and software that support lessons learned processes.

Content:

- Overview of the organization's knowledge management systems and collaborative platforms.
- Hands-on training sessions on using specific tools for capturing, storing, and retrieving lessons learned.
- Demonstrations of AI and data analytics tools that enhance lessons learned practices.
- Best practices for integrating these tools into daily project management activities.

Outcome: Participants will be proficient in using technology to streamline the lessons learned process, making it more efficient and effective.

Interactive Elements and Continuous Learning

To ensure the effectiveness of workshops and training modules, it is essential to incorporate interactive elements and promote continuous learning. Some strategies include:

- **Interactive Workshops:** Use role-playing, group discussions, and case study analyses to engage participants and reinforce learning.

- **Regular Refreshers:** Offer periodic refresher courses and advanced training sessions to keep team members updated on best practices and new tools.

- **Mentorship Programs:** Pair experienced project managers with new team members to provide guidance and support in applying lessons learned.

- **Feedback Loops:** Collect feedback from participants to continuously improve the training program and address emerging needs.

By implementing comprehensive workshops and training modules, organizations can build a knowledgeable and skilled workforce committed to capturing, analyzing, and applying lessons learned. This, in turn, fosters a culture of continuous improvement and drives better project outcomes.

ALEX'S EXPERIENCE WITH TRAINING PROGRAMS

Alex organized regular training sessions to educate team members on the principles of lessons learned and how to use the knowledge management system effectively. These sessions included hands-on workshops where team members practiced capturing and analyzing lessons.

Implementing Lessons Learned in Project Phases

Integrating lessons learned into every phase of a project ensures continuous improvement and knowledge sharing. This proactive approach helps in avoiding past mistakes, leveraging successful strategies, and enhancing overall project performance. Here's how to implement lessons learned throughout the project lifecycle:

1. Initiation Phase: Review Lessons from Past Projects to Inform Project Planning

Objective: To lay a strong foundation for the project by incorporating insights from previous projects.

Actions:

◊ Conduct a thorough review of documented lessons learned from similar past projects.

◊ Identify relevant lessons that can influence project scope, objectives, and stakeholder expectations.

◊ Engage with team members who were involved in past projects to gain additional insights and contextual understanding.

Outcome: Project planning is informed by historical data, leading to better-defined objectives and realistic expectations.

2. Planning Phase: Identify Potential Risks and Opportunities Based on Previous Lessons

Objective: To anticipate and mitigate risks while identifying opportunities for improvement based on past experiences.

Actions:

◊ Use lessons learned to identify potential risks encountered in similar projects and develop mitigation strategies.

◊ Leverage successful strategies and best practices from past projects to identify opportunities for efficiency and innovation.

◊ Integrate lessons learned into the project risk management plan and contingency plans.

◊ Ensure that the project schedule, budget, and resource allocation reflect insights from previous lessons.

Outcome: A comprehensive and proactive project plan that addresses potential risks and leverages opportunities for success.

3. Execution Phase: Conduct Regular Debriefings and Capture Lessons in Real-Time

Objective: To continuously capture and apply lessons learned during project execution.

Actions:

◊ Schedule regular debriefing sessions, such as weekly or bi-weekly meetings, to discuss ongoing challenges and successes.

◊ Encourage team members to document lessons learned in real-time using standardized templates and tools.

◊ Foster an open and transparent environment where team members feel comfortable sharing their experiences and insights.

◊ Apply relevant lessons immediately to ongoing project activities to improve performance and address issues.

Outcome: Continuous capture and application of lessons learned, leading to real-time improvements and adaptive project management.

4. Monitoring and Controlling Phase: Analyze Lessons to Adjust Project Plans and Mitigate Risks

Objective: To use lessons learned to make informed adjustments to project plans and control processes.

Actions:

◊ Regularly review captured lessons and analyze their impact on project performance metrics.

◊ Adjust project plans, schedules, and resource allocations based on insights from lessons learned.

◊ Implement corrective actions to address identified issues and mitigate emerging risks.

◊ Use data analytics to track the effectiveness of applied lessons and make further refinements as needed.

Outcome: Dynamic and responsive project management that continuously adapts to changing conditions and emerging insights.

5. Closing Phase: Conduct a Final Lessons Learned Session to Document and Share Insights

Objective: To comprehensively review and document lessons learned at the end of the project.

Actions:

◊ Organize a final lessons learned session with all project stakeholders to discuss the project's successes, challenges, and areas for improvement.

◊ Document all insights in a structured and detailed lessons learned report.

◊ Share the final lessons learned report with the wider organization to contribute to the organizational knowledge base.

◊ Identify actionable recommendations for future projects based on the documented lessons.

Outcome: A comprehensive lessons learned report that captures valuable insights and contributes to the continuous improvement of future projects.

Benefits of Integrating Lessons Learned Throughout the Project Lifecycle

By embedding lessons learned into each phase of the project lifecycle, organizations can achieve several benefits:

1. **Enhanced Project Planning:** Lessons learned from past projects provide a rich source of information that can improve project planning and prevent common pitfalls.

2. **Proactive Risk Management:** Identifying potential risks and opportunities early in the project lifecycle allows for more effective risk management and contingency planning.

3. **Continuous Improvement:** Regular debriefings and real-time documentation of lessons ensure that improvements are continuously identified and applied throughout the project.

4. **Adaptive Project Management:** Analyzing lessons during the monitoring and controlling phase enables project managers to make informed adjustments and respond to changing conditions effectively.

5. **Knowledge Sharing:** Documenting and sharing lessons learned during the closing phase contributes to the organizational knowledge base, fostering a culture of continuous learning and improvement.

By systematically integrating lessons learned into each phase of the project lifecycle, organizations can enhance their project management practices, drive better project outcomes, and build a culture of continuous improvement and knowledge sharing. Alex's journey in implementing these practices demonstrates the tangible benefits of this approach, providing a roadmap for other project managers to follow.

CASE STUDY: CONSTRUCTION PROJECT LIFECYCLE

A construction company integrated lessons learned into every phase of its project lifecycle. By reviewing past lessons during project initiation and planning, the company was able to identify potential issues early and implement mitigation strategies, resulting in fewer project delays and cost overruns (Gibson Jr. et al., 2006).

ALEX'S EXPERIENCE WITH PROJECT PHASES

Alex ensured that lessons learned were integrated into every phase of the project lifecycle. During the initiation phase, Alex reviewed lessons from similar projects to inform planning. Throughout execution, Alex conducted regular debriefings to capture lessons in real-time. This proactive approach led to more informed decision-making and improved project outcomes.

Case Studies and Examples of Successful Implementation

1. **Manufacturing Industry:** A major manufacturing firm used lessons learned to improve its production processes. By systematically capturing and analyzing lessons from each production cycle, the firm identified inefficiencies and implemented process improvements that increased productivity by 15% (Liker, 2004).

2. **Healthcare Sector:** A hospital implemented a lessons learned process to improve patient care. By analyzing past incidents and identifying root causes, the hospital introduced new protocols that reduced medical errors by 25% (Barends et al., 2015).

3. **Finance Industry:** A financial services company used lessons learned to enhance its risk management practices. By reviewing lessons from past financial crises, the company developed more robust risk assessment models, leading to better investment decisions and reduced losses (Kerzner, 2022).

Conclusion

The practical application of lessons learned practices is essential for translating theory into action. This chapter has provided an array of tools, templates, and methodologies that project managers can use to enhance their lessons learned processes. By implementing these practical applications, project managers can ensure that lessons learned are systematically captured, analyzed, and applied, leading to continuous improvement and more successful project outcomes.

Alex's journey has underscored the importance of using practical tools to support lessons learned practices. Through the use of templates, software solutions, and collaborative platforms, Alex was able to streamline the process of capturing and sharing valuable insights. This approach not only improved efficiency but also made lessons learned more accessible and actionable for the entire team.

Key Tools and Applications

◊ **Templates:** Standardized templates provide a structured format for capturing lessons learned, ensuring consistency and completeness. Alex's use of templates facilitated the systematic documentation of insights, making it easier to analyze and apply them to future projects.

◊ **Software Solutions:** Project management software and knowledge management systems can automate data collection, storage, and retrieval, enhancing the efficiency of lessons learned practices. Alex's implementation of these tools reduced manual effort and improved data accuracy.

◊ **Collaborative Platforms:** Collaborative tools enable real-time knowledge sharing and foster a culture of continuous improvement. By using platforms that support collaboration, Alex was able to engage the entire team in the lessons learned process, promoting collective learning and innovation.

Practical Applications in Action

◊ **Alex's Implementation of Tools:** Alex's strategic use of practical tools and applications demonstrated how technology can enhance lessons learned practices. By integrating templates, software solutions, and collaborative platforms into the project management workflow, Alex was able to capture and apply lessons more effectively.

◊ **Overcoming Challenges:** The use of practical tools helped Alex overcome common challenges such as resistance to change and inconsistent documentation. By showcasing the tangible benefits of these tools, Alex was able to gain buy-in from the team and ensure the successful implementation of lessons learned practices.

Benefits of Practical Applications

◊ **Enhanced Efficiency:** Automating routine tasks and standardizing documentation processes save time and resources, allowing project managers to focus on strategic activities.

◊ **Improved Accuracy:** Tools that support data collection and analysis reduce the likelihood of human error, ensuring that lessons learned are based on accurate and reliable information.

◊ **Increased Accessibility:** Collaborative platforms and knowledge management systems make lessons learned easily accessible to all team members, fostering a culture of continuous learning and improvement.

Moving Forward

As we move forward, the next chapter will delve into the integration of artificial intelligence (AI) in lessons learned practices. AI has the potential to further enhance the efficiency and effectiveness of lessons learned processes by automating data analysis, providing predictive insights, and identifying patterns that may not be immediately obvious to human analysts.

By leveraging AI, project managers can elevate lessons learned practices to the next level, ensuring that insights are not only captured and analyzed but also used to drive proactive decision-making and continuous improvement. This integration of advanced technologies with practical tools and methodologies will provide a comprehensive approach to achieving project management excellence.

The practical application of lessons learned practices is crucial for translating theoretical concepts into tangible improvements. By using standardized templates, software solutions, and collaborative platforms, project managers can enhance the efficiency, accuracy, and accessibility of lessons learned processes. Alex's journey has demonstrated the transformative impact of these tools, providing a roadmap for other project managers to follow. As you continue to explore the subsequent chapters, you will gain deeper insights and tools to further enhance your lessons learned practices, ensuring that your organization can achieve sustainable success through continuous learning and adaptation.

Chapter Insights

_____

_____

_____

_____

_____

_____

_____

_____

_____

_____

_____

_____

_____

_____

CHAPTER 8

Lessons Learned and Artificial Intelligence

Introduction to Artificial Intelligence in Project Management

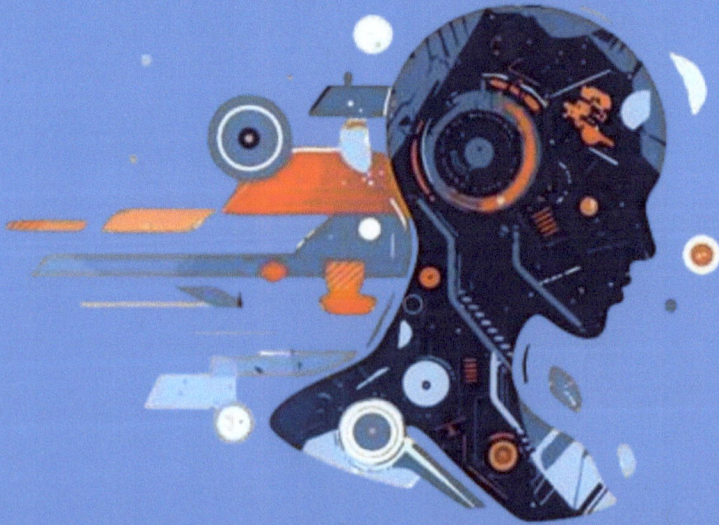

Artificial Intelligence (AI) has become a transformative force in various industries, including project management. AI can significantly enhance lessons learned practices by automating data collection, analysis, and insights generation. This chapter explores how AI can be integrated into lessons learned processes, providing project managers like Alex with advanced tools to improve project outcomes.

The Role of AI in Lessons Learned

AI technologies can streamline and enhance lessons learned practices in several ways:

1. **Automated Data Collection:** AI can automatically collect data from various sources, including project management tools, emails, and documents, reducing the manual effort required for data gathering. This automation ensures that data is collected consistently and comprehensively, providing a solid foundation for analysis. By integrating AI into project management systems, organizations can capture a wide array of data points, from task completion times to communication logs, ensuring that all relevant information is available for lessons learned.

2. **Natural Language Processing (NLP):** NLP algorithms can analyze textual data, extracting key insights and trends from project reports, meeting notes, and feedback forms. This capability allows AI to understand and interpret human language, identifying significant themes and recurring issues that might be buried in vast amounts of text. For instance, NLP can highlight frequent mentions of specific problems or successes across multiple projects, providing valuable insights that inform future project planning and execution.

3. **Predictive Analytics:** AI can use historical data to predict future project risks and opportunities, helping project managers make proactive decisions. By analyzing past project data, AI can identify patterns that indicate potential risks, such as schedule delays or budget overruns. Predictive analytics can also forecast positive outcomes, allowing project managers to leverage best practices and strategies that have led to success in similar projects. This forward-looking approach enables better risk management and strategic planning.

4. **Pattern Recognition:** AI can identify patterns and correlations in data that might be missed by human analysts, providing deeper insights into project performance and outcomes. For example, AI can analyze the correlation between team communication frequency and project success rates or identify which project phases are most prone to delays. These insights can help project managers pinpoint areas for improvement and implement targeted strategies to enhance project efficiency and effectiveness.

5. **Real-Time Monitoring:** AI tools can provide real-time monitoring and alerts, ensuring that lessons learned are applied during the project lifecycle, not just at the end. Real-time monitoring allows project managers to address issues as they arise rather than waiting until a project is completed to analyze what went wrong. AI-driven alerts can notify project managers of deviations from the plan, such as exceeding budget thresholds or falling behind on critical tasks, enabling immediate corrective actions.

CASE STUDY: AI IN CONSTRUCTION PROJECT MANAGEMENT

A construction company implemented an AI-powered project management tool to enhance its lessons learned process. The AI system collected data from project reports, schedules, and communications, identifying patterns and potential risks. By using predictive analytics, the company was able to forecast project delays and cost overruns, taking corrective actions early. This proactive approach led to a 15% improvement in project completion times and a 10% reduction in costs (Ekinci, 2020).

Predictive Analytics and Risk Management

AI models, such as Extreme Learning Machines (ELM), have proven effective in predicting construction project costs and delays by analyzing risk factors and delay factors. These models use historical project data to identify potential issues and provide accurate forecasts, enabling project managers to take preemptive actions (Ali & Abd, 2021).

Enhancing Efficiency with AI

AI applications in construction management can significantly reduce human intervention in repetitive and rule-based tasks. Rathod and Sonawane (2022) demonstrated that AI-based solutions, such as Artificial Neural Networks (ANN) and Support Vector Machines (SVM), effectively manage financial aspects and time scheduling in construction projects. These technologies help identify and mitigate delays and cost overruns, leading to more efficient project management (Rathod & Sonawane, 2022).

AI in Change Management

AI-based prediction systems for change management in construction projects can proactively manage changes that lead to delays and cost overruns. Zhao et al. (2010) presented a change prediction system using activity- based dependency structure matrix (DSM) and Monte Carlo simulation. This system helps project managers predict and manage changes efficiently, thus minimizing disruptions and improving project outcomes (Zhao et al., 2010).

Impact on Project Performance

The integration of AI in construction project management leads to significant improvements in project performance. A study by Aung et al. (2023) highlighted the superior predictive accuracy of machine learning algorithms in forecasting cost overruns, enabling better planning, risk mitigation, and stakeholder satisfaction. The study found that machine learning approaches provide a reliable strategy for managing construction costs, leading to more efficient and financially sound project management practices (Aung et al., 2023).

The implementation of AI-powered project management tools in construction enhances the lessons learned process, improves efficiency, and reduces costs. By leveraging predictive analytics, construction companies can proactively address potential risks, leading to better project outcomes and overall performance improvements.

ALEX'S EXPERIENCE WITH AI INTEGRATION

◊ **Automated Data Collection:** Alex implemented an AI-powered tool that automatically gathered data from various project management systems and communication platforms. This tool significantly reduced the time spent on manual data entry and ensured that all relevant information was captured accurately and promptly.

◊ **Natural Language Processing (NLP):** By using NLP algorithms, Alex was able to analyze meeting transcripts and project documentation to identify recurring issues and positive outcomes. This analysis provided valuable insights into team dynamics and project performance that were previously overlooked.

- ◊ **Predictive Analytics:** Alex leveraged AI-driven predictive analytics to forecast potential project risks based on historical data. This capability allowed the team to implement proactive measures to mitigate risks before they could impact the project significantly. By using AI-driven predictive analytics, Alex was able to anticipate potential project risks and adjust plans accordingly, reducing the likelihood of project overruns.

- ◊ **Pattern Recognition:** AI tools helped Alex identify patterns in project data, such as common causes of delays and budget overruns. By understanding these patterns, Alex was able to develop strategies to address these issues in future projects, leading to more efficient project execution.

- ◊ **Real-Time Monitoring:** With AI-enabled real-time monitoring, Alex received instant alerts about potential issues, such as deviations from the project schedule or budget. This real-time feedback allowed the team to make immediate adjustments, ensuring that projects stayed on track.

Behavioral Science Insight: Overcoming Cognitive Biases with AI

AI can help mitigate cognitive biases by providing objective data and analysis. For example, AI can counteract optimism bias by providing realistic project timelines based on historical data. Similarly, AI can reduce confirmation bias by presenting diverse perspectives and insights that may challenge existing beliefs (Ramirez & De Baets, 2021).

AI offers a range of powerful tools and techniques that can significantly enhance lessons learned practices in project management. Here are some specific applications of AI in this area:

1. Text Mining and Natural Language Processing (NLP): AI can analyze large volumes of text data from project reports, feedback forms, and emails, extracting key lessons and insights. NLP algorithms can identify common themes, patterns, and sentiments, providing a comprehensive view of project experiences. For instance, NLP can process meeting notes to highlight frequently discussed issues or positive outcomes, giving project managers a clearer understanding of the team's challenges and successes (Manning et al., 2008). This technology can also detect sentiment trends, such as rising frustration or satisfaction, which can be critical for addressing team morale and project dynamics in real-time.

2. Predictive Modeling: AI can use historical project data to build predictive models, forecasting future risks and opportunities. These models help project managers anticipate potential issues and take proactive measures to mitigate them. For example, by analyzing past projects, AI can predict the likelihood of budget overruns or schedule delays based on current project metrics. This foresight enables project managers to allocate resources more effectively and implement risk mitigation strategies before problems escalate (Frost & Sullivan, 2019). Predictive modeling can also identify opportunities for improvement by highlighting practices that have consistently led to successful outcomes.

3. Recommendation Systems: AI can generate recommendations based on historical data and patterns, suggesting best practices and potential improvements for future projects. Recommendation systems can analyze a vast array of data points to provide actionable insights tailored to specific project contexts. For instance, if a particular project faces

challenges with stakeholder communication, the AI system might recommend more frequent updates or the use of collaborative tools to enhance transparency and engagement (Aggarwal, 2016). These personalized recommendations help project managers apply proven strategies and avoid repeating past mistakes.

4. Automated Reporting: AI can automate the creation of lessons learned reports, summarizing key insights and recommendations. This automation saves time and ensures that lessons are consistently documented and shared across the organization. AI-driven reporting tools can compile data from various sources, analyze it, and generate comprehensive reports that highlight significant findings and actionable steps. Automated reporting not only streamlines the documentation process but also enhances the accuracy and consistency of the information shared, making it easier for teams to access and apply the lessons learned (Chui et al., 2018).

ALEX'S EXPERIENCE WITH AI APPLICATIONS

Text Mining and NLP

◊ **Implementation:** Alex utilized NLP tools to analyze feedback forms and project documentation. This analysis identified recurring themes, such as communication issues and resource constraints, providing actionable insights.

◊ **Outcome:** The insights gained through NLP helped Alex address specific team concerns and improve communication strategies, leading to more cohesive project execution.

Predictive Modeling

◊ **Implementation:** Alex integrated predictive modeling tools to forecast potential risks based on historical project data. The models predicted budget overruns and schedule delays, allowing Alex to take proactive measures.

◊ **Outcome:** By anticipating these risks, Alex could allocate resources more effectively and implement mitigation strategies, resulting in smoother project execution and fewer surprises.

Recommendation Systems

◊ **Implementation:** Alex employed AI-driven recommendation systems to suggest best practices for upcoming projects. The system provided tailored recommendations based on past project data and current project specifics.

◊ **Outcome:** These recommendations helped Alex implement strategies that had been successful in similar contexts, improving project outcomes and team efficiency.

Automated Reporting

◊ **Implementation:** Alex used AI tools to automate the generation of lessons learned reports. The system compiled and analyzed data, creating detailed reports that highlighted key insights and actionable recommendations.

◊ **Outcome:** Automated reporting saved significant time and ensured that lessons were consistently documented and easily accessible, fostering a culture of continuous improvement.

The applications of AI in lessons learned practices provide project managers with advanced tools to enhance data collection, analysis, and decision-making. By leveraging technologies such as text mining, predictive modeling, recommendation systems, and automated reporting, project managers like Alex can gain deeper insights, anticipate risks, and implement effective strategies to improve project outcomes. These AI-driven capabilities streamline the lessons learned process and foster a more proactive and data-driven approach to project management, driving continuous improvement and organizational success.

CASE STUDY: AI IN IT PROJECT MANAGEMENT

A global IT company used AI to enhance its lessons learned process. The AI system analyzed project data, identifying common issues such as scope creep and communication breakdowns. By providing real-time insights and recommendations, the AI tool helped project managers address these issues proactively. This led to a 20% increase in project success rates and improved client satisfaction.

Managing Scope Creep with AI

Scope creep, the uncontrolled expansion of a product or project scope without adjustments to time, cost, and resources, is a significant risk in IT projects. Effective management of scope creep is critical for project success. Althiyabi and Qureshi (2021) emphasized the importance of defining a clear statement of work and improving communication between clients and development teams to prevent scope creep. Their proposed method includes regular monitoring and adjustment of project scope to maintain control and enhance project outcomes (Althiyabi & Qureshi, 2021).

Addressing Communication Breakdowns

Effective communication is crucial for the success of IT projects. Naqvi and Aziz (2011) found that poor stakeholder communication management leads to issues such as scope creep, cost overruns, and schedule delays. They recommended ensuring high-quality stakeholder communication as a primary tool for determining project scope, time, and cost. Improved communication management significantly enhances project outcomes and stakeholder satisfaction (Naqvi & Aziz, 2011).

Benefits of AI in Project Management

Using AI in project management provides numerous benefits, including the ability to predict and mitigate risks proactively. A study by Komal et al. (2020) demonstrated that identifying factors contributing to scope creep through systematic literature review and empirical studies can significantly reduce its impact on project success. Their findings underscore the value of AI in analyzing large datasets to provide actionable insights and enhance project management practices (Komal et al., 2020).

Implementing AI in IT project management enhances the lessons learned process by identifying and addressing common issues such as scope creep and communication breakdowns. This proactive approach improves project success rates and client satisfaction, demonstrating the significant value of AI in managing complex IT projects.

Benefits of AI in Lessons Learned

Integrating AI into lessons learned practices offers numerous benefits that can significantly enhance project management outcomes:

1. **Enhanced Accuracy:** AI reduces human error and subjectivity, providing more accurate and reliable insights. Traditional methods of capturing lessons learned can be influenced by individual biases and memory

limitations, leading to incomplete or skewed data. However, AI algorithms analyze data consistently and objectively, ensuring that insights are based on factual information rather than subjective interpretations. This enhanced accuracy helps project managers make better-informed decisions, leading to improved project performance (Chui et al., 2018).

2. **Increased Efficiency:** AI automates data collection and analysis, saving time and resources for project teams. Manual processes of gathering and analyzing data can be time-consuming and labor-intensive. AI tools streamline these tasks, quickly processing large volumes of data and identifying key patterns and insights. This automation allows project teams to focus on higher-value activities, such as implementing improvements and strategizing for future projects, rather than getting bogged down in data handling (Manyika et al., 2017).

3. **Proactive Decision-Making:** AI provides predictive insights, enabling project managers to take proactive measures and mitigate risks. By analyzing historical project data, AI can forecast potential issues before they arise, allowing project managers to develop mitigation strategies in advance. This proactive approach helps prevent project delays, budget overruns, and other common challenges, leading to smoother project execution and better outcomes (Bughin et al., 2017).

4. **Scalability:** AI can handle large volumes of data, making it scalable for organizations of all sizes and project complexities. Whether managing a small project or a large portfolio of projects, AI systems can efficiently process and analyze vast amounts of information. This scalability ensures that organizations can leverage AI's capabilities regardless of their size or the complexity of their projects, providing consistent and reliable insights across the board (Aggarwal, 2016).

Challenges and Considerations

While AI offers significant benefits, there are also challenges and considerations to keep in mind:

1. **Data Quality:** The effectiveness of AI depends on the quality of the data. Ensuring accurate, consistent, and comprehensive data is crucial for reliable AI insights. Poor data quality can lead to incorrect conclusions and flawed decision-making. Organizations must invest in robust data governance practices, including data validation, cleansing, and standardization, to ensure that the data fed into AI systems is of high quality (Manning et al., 2008).

2. **Integration:** Integrating AI tools with existing project management systems can be complex and requires careful planning and execution. Seamless integration ensures that AI systems can access and process relevant data without disruptions. However, this process may involve technical challenges, such as compatibility issues and data migration. Organizations need to develop a clear integration strategy and work closely with technology providers to address these challenges effectively (Chui et al., 2018).

3. **Ethical Considerations:** Ensuring that AI systems are used ethically and transparently is important for maintaining trust and avoiding biases in decision-making. AI algorithms can inadvertently perpetuate biases present in the training data, leading to unfair or discriminatory outcomes. Organizations must implement ethical guidelines for AI use, including regular audits, transparency in AI processes, and efforts to mitigate biases. This approach helps build trust among stakeholders and ensures that AI systems are used responsibly (Ramirez & De Baets, 2021).

4. **Skills and Training:** Project managers and teams need training to effectively use AI tools and interpret AI-generated insights. Without proper understanding and skills, teams may struggle to leverage AI's full potential. Organizations should invest in training programs that equip project managers with the knowledge to operate AI tools, understand their outputs, and integrate these insights into decision-making processes. Continuous learning and skill development are essential for maximizing the benefits of AI in project management (Manyika et al., 2017).

The integration of AI into lessons learned practices offers significant benefits, including enhanced accuracy, increased efficiency, proactive decision-making, and scalability. However, to fully realize these benefits, organizations must address challenges related to data quality, integration, ethical considerations, and skills training. By taking a strategic approach to implementing AI, project managers can harness its potential to drive continuous improvement and achieve better project outcomes.

Conclusion

Integrating artificial intelligence (AI) into lessons learned practices represents a significant leap forward in the field of project management. AI technologies can streamline and enhance the process of capturing, analyzing, and applying lessons learned, providing project managers with powerful tools to improve project outcomes. This chapter has explored various applications of AI in lessons learned, demonstrating how these technologies can be leveraged to drive continuous improvement and innovation.

Alex's journey has highlighted the transformative potential of AI in lessons learned practices. By implementing AI-driven tools, Alex was able to automate data collection, perform advanced data analysis, and generate predictive insights, all of which contributed to more efficient and effective project management.

◊ **Automated Data Collection:** AI can automatically gather data from various sources, reducing the manual effort required and ensuring comprehensive data capture. Alex's use of AI-driven tools for data collection streamlined the process and improved data accuracy.

◊ **Natural Language Processing (NLP):** NLP algorithms can analyze textual data from project reports, feedback forms, and emails to extract key insights and identify common themes. Alex leveraged NLP to gain deeper insights into project performance and team dynamics.

◊ **Predictive Analytics:** AI can use historical project data to build predictive models that forecast future risks and opportunities. This capability allowed Alex to anticipate potential issues and take proactive measures to mitigate risks.

◊ **Pattern Recognition:** AI can identify patterns and correlations in data that human analysts might miss. Alex used AI-driven pattern recognition to uncover hidden trends and inform strategic decision-making.

◊ **Real-Time Monitoring:** AI tools can provide real-time monitoring and alerts, ensuring that lessons learned are applied during the project lifecycle, not just at the end. Alex's implementation of real-time AI monitoring helped address issues promptly and maintain project alignment.

◊ **Enhanced Accuracy:** AI reduces human error and subjectivity, providing more accurate and reliable insights. Alex's reliance on AI-driven analysis ensured that lessons learned were based on solid evidence.

◊ **Increased Efficiency:** Automating data collection and analysis saves time and resources, allowing project teams to focus on strategic activities. Alex's use of AI tools significantly improved the efficiency of lessons learned processes.

◊ **Proactive Decision-Making:** AI provides predictive insights that enable project managers to take proactive measures and mitigate risks. Alex's ability to anticipate and address potential issues early on led to smoother project execution.

◊ **Scalability:** AI can handle large volumes of data, making it scalable for organizations of all sizes and project complexities. Alex's implementation of AI tools demonstrated their scalability and adaptability to different project contexts.

ALEX'S EXPERIENCE WITH AI INTEGRATION

Alex's journey with AI integration serves as a compelling example of how advanced technologies can enhance lessons learned practices. By leveraging AI tools, Alex was able to automate routine tasks, gain deeper insights, and make more informed decisions. This integration improved project outcomes and fostered a culture of innovation and continuous improvement within the team.

Moving Forward

As we move forward, the final chapter will summarize the key takeaways from the book and provide a call to action for project managers and organizations. It will emphasize the importance of continuous learning and adaptation, highlighting the need for ongoing commitment to lessons learned practices and the integration of advanced technologies.

By combining structured frameworks, evidence-based management, behavioral science insights, practical tools, and AI technologies, project managers can create a comprehensive approach to lessons learned that drives continuous improvement and project success. Alex's journey has provided valuable lessons and practical examples that can guide other project managers on their path to excellence.

Integrating AI into lessons learned practices offers a powerful approach to enhancing project management capabilities. By leveraging AI technologies, project managers can automate data collection and analysis, gain predictive insights, and identify patterns that drive proactive decision- making and continuous improvement. Alex's journey serves as a testament to the transformative potential of AI, providing a roadmap for other project managers to follow. As you reflect on the insights and tools presented in this book, consider how you can integrate AI and other advanced technologies into your lessons learned practices to achieve sustainable success through continuous learning and adaptation.

Chapter Insights

_____

_____

_____

_____

_____

_____

_____

_____

_____

_____

_____

_____

_____

_____

CHAPTER 9
Conclusion

Implementing effective lessons learned practices is an ongoing journey that requires commitment from both project managers and organizations. By understanding the importance of lessons learned, recognizing common challenges, and adopting structured frameworks, organizations can significantly enhance their project management capabilities and drive continuous improvement.

Alex's Journey Summarized

Alex's journey throughout this book highlights the transformative potential of lessons learned practices. Initially facing challenges such as resistance to change and a lack of time, Alex demonstrated perseverance and strategic thinking in implementing the Project Integrated Lessons Learned (PILL) Framework. By gaining leadership support and fostering a culture of continuous improvement, Alex was able to systematically capture, analyze, and apply lessons learned, leading to better project outcomes and enhanced team performance.

Key Takeaways

1. Understanding the Importance of Lessons Learned:
◊ Lessons learned are crucial for avoiding past mistakes, replicating successes, and driving continuous improvement.
◊ Effective lessons learned practices contribute to better project outcomes, higher efficiency, and increased stakeholder satisfaction.

2. Overcoming Challenges:
◊ Common challenges include resistance to change, lack of time, inconsistent application, and insufficient leadership support.

◊   Addressing these challenges requires strong leadership, formal processes, technology integration, and regular training.

3. Structured Frameworks and Methodologies:

◊   The PILL Framework provides a comprehensive approach to capturing, analyzing, and applying lessons learned.

◊   Other methodologies, such as evidence-based management and behavioral science insights, enhance the effectiveness of lessons learned practices.

4. Behavioral Science Insights:

◊   Understanding cognitive biases and team dynamics is crucial for implementing practical lessons learned practices.

◊   Strategies to mitigate biases and foster a culture of continuous improvement enhance the overall impact of lessons learned.

5. Practical Tools and Applications:

◊   Utilizing templates, software solutions, and collaborative platforms streamlines the lessons learned process.

◊   AI technologies can further enhance the efficiency and effectiveness of lessons learned practices by automating data analysis and providing predictive insights.

6. Organizational Culture:

◊   A supportive organizational culture that values continuous learning and knowledge sharing is essential for the success of lessons learned practices.

◊   Leadership commitment, clear communication channels, and an environment of psychological safety foster a culture conducive to lessons learned.

As project management continues to evolve, the integration of advanced technologies and methodologies will further enhance the effectiveness of lessons learned practices. Future directions include:

1. Advanced Analytics and AI:
◊ Continued development and integration of AI and machine learning technologies will provide deeper insights and more accurate predictions, further enhancing the lessons learned process.

2. Cross-Functional Collaboration:
◊ Encouraging collaboration across different teams and departments will lead to more innovative solutions and improvements by leveraging a broader range of experiences and knowledge.

3. Global Knowledge Sharing:
◊ Establishing global knowledge-sharing platforms and networks will enable organizations to learn from each other's experiences, fostering a culture of continuous improvement on a larger scale.

4. Sustainability and Adaptability:
◊ Emphasizing sustainability and adaptability in lessons learned practices will ensure that organizations remain resilient and capable of thriving in dynamic and uncertain environments.

Call to Action

The journey of implementing effective lessons learned practices is ongoing and requires commitment from both project managers and organizations. By understanding the importance of lessons learned, recognizing common challenges, and adopting structured frameworks, organizations can significantly enhance their project management capabilities and drive continuous improvement. Alex's story illustrates the transformative potential of these practices, providing a roadmap for other project managers to follow. As you apply the insights and tools presented in this book, remember that the goal is to capture lessons learned and create a culture of continuous learning and improvement that will drive long-term success.

Conclusion Recap

In summary, this book has provided a comprehensive guide to lessons learned practices, supported by evidence-based management principles, real-life examples, advanced methodologies, and insights from behavioral science. By following the journey of Alex, a seasoned project manager, readers have gained practical, real-world examples of how to overcome common barriers and successfully embed lessons learned into the project management process. As you continue your journey, remember that the key to success lies in the continuous application and refinement of these practices, fostering a culture of learning and innovation within your organization.

Glossary

After-Action Review (AAR) – A structured debriefing process conducted after project phases or significant events to discuss what happened, why it happened, and how it can be improved in the future.

Artificial Intelligence (AI) – The simulation of human intelligence in machines that are programmed to think and learn. In project management, AI can automate data collection and analysis and generate insights.

Behavioral Science – The study of human behavior, including how people make decisions and interact in groups. In project management, it helps understand cognitive biases and social dynamics affecting team performance.

Benchmarking – The process of comparing project practices, performance, or outcomes against industry standards or best practices to identify areas for improvement. Benchmarking is used to assess the effectiveness of lessons learned processes.

Cognitive Bias – A systematic pattern of deviation from norm or rationality in judgment, which can affect decision-making and project outcomes (Ramirez & De Baets, 2021).

Confirmation Bias – The tendency to search for, interpret, and remember information in a way that confirms one's preconceptions (Ramirez & De Baets, 2021).

Cross-Functional Collaboration – The process of integrating and aligning diverse team members or departments to leverage their collective expertise in achieving project goals.

Data-Driven Decision Making – The process of making decisions based on data analysis and interpretation rather than intuition or observation alone.

Evidence-Based Management (EBM) – An approach that involves making decisions and managing projects based on the best available evidence from multiple sources, including empirical data and scientific research.

Feedback Loops – Systems that use the results of a process or activity to adjust and improve the process itself, commonly used in iterative project management methodologies.

Heuristics – Mental shortcuts or rules of thumb that people use to make decisions quickly and efficiently. While heuristics can simplify complex decision-making processes, they can also lead to cognitive biases and errors in judgment. In project management, understanding heuristics is important for recognizing potential biases that may affect the lessons learned process and implementing strategies to mitigate their impact (Ramirez & De Baets, 2021).

Knowledge Management System (KMS) – A technology platform used to store, share, and manage knowledge within an organization, making it easily accessible to all team members.

Lessons Learned – Insights gained from the experiences of past projects, including both successes and failures, used to improve future project performance. Also defined as "the knowledge gained during a project, which shows how project events were addressed or should be addressed in the future, for the purpose of improving future performance" (Project Management Institute, 2021, p. 242).

Natural Language Processing (NLP) – A field of AI that enables machines to understand and interpret human language. In project management, NLP can analyze textual data from reports, feedback forms, and emails to extract insights.

Optimism Bias - The tendency to overestimate the likelihood of positive outcomes and underestimate the likelihood of negative ones (Ramirez & De Baets, 2021).

Organizational Culture - A complex, multi-dimensional phenomenon wherein a group develops in a manner to cope with problems and allows organizational members to develop their own ideologies, goals, and actions (Bhaduri, 2019).

Predictive Analytics - The use of data, statistical algorithms, and machine learning techniques to identify the likelihood of future outcomes based on historical data.

Project Integrated Lessons Learned (PILL) Framework™ - A structured methodology for capturing, analyzing, and applying lessons learned throughout the project lifecycle.

Project Success - A project's ability to impact an organization as a product, how the final product is received by the stakeholders in terms of quality, and how the project is finished in terms of budget, scope, and time (Sulistiyani and Tyas, 2022). It is also defined as the completion of a project at each time, within a given budget, and "the result of the project ultimately satisfies the end user" (Irfan and Hassan, 2019).

Psychological Safety - A belief that one will not be punished or humiliated for speaking up with ideas, questions, concerns, or mistakes, fostering an open and collaborative team environment.

Reflective Practices - Regular activities that encourage individuals or teams to think critically about their actions and decisions, aiming to identify areas for improvement.

Risk Appetite - The amount and type of risk an organization is willing to accept to achieve its objectives.

Root Cause Analysis (RCA) – A problem-solving method used to identify the underlying causes of issues or successes, often using techniques such as the "5 Whys" or fishbone diagrams.

Scenario Panning – A strategic tool used to anticipate and prepare for potential future events by exploring and analyzing various hypothetical scenarios.

Status Quo Bias – The preference for the current state of affairs and resistance to change, which can hinder the adoption of new practices (Ramirez & De Baets, 2021).

Team Dynamics - The behavioral relationships between members of a team, including how they interact and work together to achieve project goals.

Template – A pre-designed document or tool that provides a structured format for capturing and documenting information, ensuring consistency and completeness.

Transformational Leadership – A leadership style that inspires and motivates team members to achieve their full potential and contribute to the organization's success.

Reference List

Abdulmouti, H. (2015). The role of kaizen (continuous improvement) in improving companies' performance: A case study. *International Conference on Industrial Engineering and Operations Management (IEOM)*. 2015 International Conference on Industrial Engineering and Operations Management (IEOM), Dubai, United Arab Emirates. https://doi.org/10.1109/ieom.2015.7093768

Aggarwal, C. C. (2016). *Recommender systems: The textbook*. Springer. https://doi.org/10.1007/978-3-319-29659-3

Agnihothri, S., & Agnihothri, R. (2018). Application of evidence-based management to chronic disease healthcare: A framework. *Management Decision*, *56*(10), 2125-2147. https://doi.org/10.1108/md-10-2017-1010

Ahlstrom, D., Lamond, D., & Ding, Z. (2009). Reexamining some management lessons from military history. *Asia Pacific Journal of Management*, *26*(4), 617– 642. https://doi.org/10.1007/s10490-009-9155-2

Akgün, A. E., Keskin, H., Byrne, J. C., & Günsel, A. (2011). Antecedents and results of emotional capability in software development project teams. *Journal of Product Innovation Management*, *28*(6), 957-973. https://doi.org/10.1111/j.1540-5885.2011.00845.x

Almeida, M. V., & Soares, A. L. (2014). Knowledge sharing in project-based organizations: Overcoming the informational limbo. *International Journal of Information Management*, *34*(6), 770-779. https://doi.org/10.1016/j.ijinfomgt.2014.07.003

Althiyabi, T., & Qureshi, R. (2021). Predefined project scope changes and its causes for project success. *International Journal of Software Engineering & Applications*, *12*(3), 45-56. https://doi.org/10.5121/ijsea.2021.12304

Arditi, D., Polat, G., & Akin, S. (2010). Lessons learned system in construction management. *International Journal of Project Organisation and Management*, 2(1), 61–83. https://doi.org/10.1504/ijpom.2010.031882

Asch, S. E. (1956). Studies of independence and conformity: A minority of one against a unanimous majority. *Psychological Monographs: General and Applied*, 70(9), 1–70. https://doi.org/10.1037/h0093718

Barends, E., & Rousseau, D. M. (2018). *Evidence-based management: How to use evidence to make better organizational decisions*. Kogan Page Ltd.

Barends, E., Rousseau, D., & Briner, R. (2014). Evidence-Based management, the basic principles. In *In Search of Evidence Empirical Findings and Professional Perspectives on Evidence-Based Management* (pp. 203–220). Center for Evidence-Based Management. https://research.vu.nl/ws/portalfiles/portal/42141986/complete+dissertation.pdf#page=203

Baumeister, R. F., Bratslavsky, E., Muraven, M., & Tice, D. M. (1998). Ego depletion: Is the active self a limited resource? *Journal of Personality and Social Psychology*, 74(5), 1252–1265. https://doi.org/10.1037//0022-3514.74.5.1252

Bhaduri, R. M. (2019). Leveraging culture and leadership in crisis management. *European Journal of Training and Development*, 43(5/6), 554–569. https://doi.org/10.1108/ejtd-10-2018-0109

Briner, R. B., Denyer, D., & Rousseau, D. M. (2009). Evidence-Based management: Concept cleanup time? *Academy of Management Perspectives*, 23(4), 19–32. https://doi.org/10.5465/amp.2009.45590138

Bughin, J., Hazan, E., Ramaswamy, S., Chui, M., Allas, T., Dahlström, P., Henke, N., & Trench, M. (2017). Artificial intelligence: The next digital frontier? *In McKinsey & Company*. McKinsey Global Institute. https://www.mckinsey.com/ru/~/media/mckinsey/industries/advanced%2 0electronics/our%20insights/how%20artificial%20intelligence%20can%20deli ver%20real%20value%20to%20companies/mgi-artificial-intelligence-discussion-paper.pdf

Caldas, C. H., Gibson, G. E., Weerasooriya, R., & Yohe, A. M. (2009). Identification of effective management practices and technologies for lessons learned programs in the construction industry. *Journal of Construction Engineering and Management*, *135*(6), 531-539. https://doi.org/10.1061/(asce)co.1943-7862.0000011

Chui, M., Manyika, J., & Miremadi, M. (2018). What AI can and can't do (yet) for your business. *McKinsey Quarterly*, *1*, 1-13.

Collier, B., DeMarco, T., & Fearey, P. (1996). A defined process for project post mortem review. *IEEE Software*, *13*(4), 65-72. https://doi.org/10.1109/52.526833

Connor, L., Dean, J., McNett, M., Tydings, D. M., Shrout, A., Gorsuch, P. F., Moore, A., Brown, R., Melnyk, B. M., & Gallagher-Ford, L. (2023). Evidence-Based practice improves patient outcomes and healthcare system return on investment: Findings from a scoping review. *Worldviews on Evidence-Based Nursing*, *20*(1), 6-15. https://doi.org/10.1111/wvn.12621

Cunio, J. (2024). Harnessing lessons learned: The impact of knowledge management practices on project success and organizational revenue. *PM World Journal*, *13*(10), 1-26. https://pmworldlibrary.net/wp-content/uploads/2024/11/pmwj146-OctNov2024-Cunio-Harnessing-Lessons-Learned-the-Impact-of-Knowledge-Management-2.pdf

Denyer, D., Tranfield, D., & van Aken, J. E. (2008). Developing design propositions through research synthesis. *Organization Studies, 29*(3), 393-413. https://doi.org/10.1177/0170840607088020

Ditt, W., & Schlehofer, U. (1988). A project management support tool based on feedback loop technique. *Annual Review in Automatic Programming, 14*(2), 15-20. https://doi.org/10.1016/0066-4138(90)90003-a

Duffield, S., & Whitty, S. J. (2015). Developing a systemic lessons learned knowledge model for organisational learning through projects. *International Journal of Project Management, 33*(2), 311-324. https://doi.org/10.1016/j.ijproman.2014.07.004

Edmondson, A. (1999). Psychological safety and learning behavior in work teams. *Administrative Science Quarterly, 44*(2), 350-383. https://doi.org/10.2307/2666999

Edum-Fotwe, F. T., & McCaffer, R. (2000). Developing project management competency: Perspectives from the construction industry. *International Journal of Project Management, 18*(2), 111-124. https://doi.org/10.1016/s0263-7863(98)90075-8

Eken, G., Bilgin, G., Dikmen, I., & Birgonul, M. T. (2020). A lessons-learned tool for organizational learning in construction. *Automation in Construction, 110*, 102977. https://doi.org/10.1016/j.autcon.2019.102977

Eskerod, P., & Skriver, H. J. (2007). Organizational culture restraining in-House knowledge transfer between project managers a case study. *Project Management Journal, 38*(1), 110-122. https://doi.org/10.1177/875697280703800111

Fan, C.-F., & Yu, Y.-C. (2004). BBN-based software project risk management. *Journal of Systems and Software, 73*(2), 193-203. https://doi.org/10.1016/j. jss.2003.12.032

Gerstner, L. V. (2003). *Who says elephants can't dance?: Leading a great enterprise through dramatic change*. Harper Business.

Gibson Jr., G. E., Wang, Y.-R., Cho, C.-S., & Pappas, M. P. (2006). What is preproject planning, anyway? *Journal of Management in Engineering*, 22(1), 35–42. https://doi.org/10.1061/(ASCE)0742-597X(2006)22:1(35)

Godoy, L. A. (2011). Introducing engineering students to historical/cultural perspectives through story-centered on-line learning. *Creative Education*, 2(2), 63–70. https://doi.org/10.4236/ce.2011.22009

Goodman, J. L. (2023). Opportunities for team development based on lessons learned from spaceflight operations. *IEEE Aerospace Conference*. 2023 IEEE Aerospace Conference, Big Sky, MT. https://doi.org/10.1109/AERO55745.2023.10115798

Grabois, M. R. (2011). Apollo: Learning from the past, for the future. *Acta Astronautica*, *68*(7), 1353-1360. https://doi.org/10.1016/j.actaastro.2010.08.010

Hatler, C. W., Mast, D., Corderella, J., Mitchell, G., Howard, K., Aragon, J., & Bedker, D. (2006). Using evidence and process improvement strategies to enhance healthcare outcomes for the critically ill: A pilot project. *American Journal of Critical Care*, *15*(6), 549-555. https://doi.org/10.4037/ajcc2006.15.6.549

Huang, K. (1997). Capitalizing collective knowledge for winning, execution and teamwork. *Journal of Knowledge Management*, *1*(2), 149-156. https://doi.org/10.1108/eum0000000004590

Irfan, M., & Hassan, M. (2019). The effect of project governance and sustainability on project success of the public sector organizations in Pakistan. Pertanika Journal of Social Science and Humanities, 27(T),177-198. https://www.academia.edu/39007904/The_Effect_of_Project_ Governance_and_Sustainability_on_Project_Success_of_the_Public_ Sector_Organizations_in_Pakistan

Iwao, S. (2018). The diversity and reality of kaizen in toyota. In T. Fujimoto & F. Ikuine (Eds.), *Industrial Competitiveness and Design Evolution* (pp. 271-298). Springer. https://doi.org/10.1007/978-4-431-55145-4_9

Jallow, M. B., Rovelo, M., Gharaee, S. A., Dutta, S., & Askari, M. (2023). Examining the impact of team dynamics in agile project management success in software development: A systematic literature review. *IEEE International Conference on Intelligent Data Acquisition and Advanced Computing Systems: Technology and Applications*, 1-8. https://www.researchgate.net/publication/373550127_Examining_the_Imp act_of_Team_Dynamics_in_Agile_Project_Management_Success_in_Softwar e_Development_A_ Systematic_Literature_Review

Johnson, G. (2020). Memories and safety lessons learned of an Apollo Electrical Engineer. *Journal of Space Safety Engineering*, 7(1), 18-26. https://doi.org/10.1016/j.jsse.2019.12.002

Kahneman, D. (2022). *NOISE: A flaw in human judgment*. Little, Brown.

Kerzner, H. (2022). *Project management: A systems approach to planning, scheduling, and controlling* (13th ed.). John Wiley & Sons, Inc.

Komal, B., Janjua, U. I., Anwar, F., Madni, T. M., Cheema, M. F., Malik, M. N., & Shahid, A. R. (2020). The impact of scope creep on project success: An empirical investigation. *IEEE Access*, 8(1), 125755-125775. https://doi.org/10.1109/access.2020.3007098

Kotter, J. P. (1996). *Leading change*. Harvard Business School Press.

Larrère, J.-L. (2004). Risk management and lessons learned solutions for satellite product assurance. *Acta Astronautica, 55*(3-9), 811-816. https://doi.org/10.1016/j.actaastro.2004.05.016

Liker, J. K. (2004). *The Toyota way: 14 management principles from the world's greatest manufacturer*. McGraw-Hill.

Lugtenberg, M., Burgers, J. S., & Westert, G. P. (2009). Effects of evidence-based clinical practice guidelines on quality of care: A systematic review. *Quality and Safety in Health Care, 18*(5), 385-392. https://doi.org/10.1136/qshc.2008.028043

Magnier-Watanabe, R. (2011). Getting ready for kaizen: Organizational and knowledge management enablers. *Vine, 41*(4), 428-448. https://doi.org/10.1108/03055721111188520

Manning, C. D., Raghavan, P., Hinrich Schütze, & University of Cambridge. (2008). *Introduction to information retrieval*. Cambridge University Press.

Manyika, J., Chui, M., Miremadi, M., Bughin, J., George, K., Willmott, P., & Dewhurst, M. (2017, January 12). *Harnessing automation for a future that works*. McKinsey & Company; McKinsey Global Institute. https://www.mckinsey.com/featured-insights/digital-disruption/harnessing-automation-for-a-future-that-works

Melnyk, B. M., Fineout-Overholt, E., Giggleman, M., & Cruz, R. (2010). Correlates among cognitive beliefs, EBP implementation, organizational culture, cohesion and job satisfaction in evidence-based practice mentors from a community hospital system. *Nursing Outlook, 58*(6), 301-308. https://doi.org/10.1016/j.outlook.2010.06.002

Mueller, J. (2015). Formal and informal practices of knowledge sharing between project teams and enacted cultural characteristics. *Project Management Journal*, 46(1), 53-68. https://doi.org/10.1002/pmj.21471

Murray, C. A., & Catherine Bly Cox. (1989). *Apollo, the race to the moon*. Simon & Schuster.

Naqvi, I. H., & Aziz, S. (2011). The impact of stakeholder communication on project outcome. *African Journal of Business Management*, 5(14), 5824-5832. https://www.semanticscholar.org/paper/The-impact-of-stakeholder-communication-on-project-Naqvi-Aziz/edbfad32ee1f7d1a9a23b60f29dc00d50ec40b1c

National Aeronautics and Space Administration (NASA). (1999). *Mars climate orbiter mishap investigation board: Phase I report*. (pp. 1-48). Jet Propulsion Laboratory, NASA.

National Aeronautics and Space Administration (NASA). (2017). *NASA systems engineering handbook*. NASA.

Newman, J. S., & Wander, S. M. (2002). *The knowledge path to mission success: Overview of the NASA PBMA-KMS*. IEEE. https://doi.org/10.1109/RAMS.2002.981708

Nickerson, R. S. (1998). Confirmation bias: A ubiquitous phenomenon in many guises. *Review of General Psychology*, 2(2), 175-220. https://doi.org/10.1037/1089-2680.2.2.175

Nonaka, I., & Takeuchi, H. (1995). *The knowledge-creating company: How Japanese companies create the dynamics of innovation*. Oxford University Press.

Ordóñez, L., & Benson, L. (1997). Decisions under time pressure: How time constraint affects risky decision making. *Organizational Behavior and Human Decision Processes, 71*(2), 121-140. https://doi.org/10.1006/obhd.1997.2717

Owen, D. B. (2010). Apollo spacecraft propulsion systems design philosophies. *AIAA*. AIAA Space 2010 Conference & Exposition, Anaheim, CA. https://doi.org/10.2514/6.2010-8813

Pfeffer, J., & Sutton, R. I. (2006). *Hard facts, dangerous half-truths, and total nonsense: Profiting from evidence-based management.* Harvard Business School Press.

Project Management Institute (PMI). (2021). *Guide to the project management body of knowledge.* (7th ed.). Project Management Institute.

Ramirez, J., & De Baets, S. (2021). *NeuralPlan* (J. Bull-Wilson, Ed.; 1st ed.). The Institute for Neuro & Behavioral Project Management.

Rousseau, D. M. (2006). Is there such a thing as "evidence-based management"?. *Academy of Management Review, 31*(2), 256-269. https://doi.org/10.5465/amr.2006.20208679

Samuelson, W., & Zeckhauser, R. (1988). Status quo bias in decision making. *Journal of Risk and Uncertainty, 1*(1), 7-59. https://doi.org/10.1007/bf00055564

Schein, E. H. (2017). *Organizational culture and leadership* (5th ed.). Hoboken, New Jersey Wiley. (Original work published 1985)

Schmidt, E., & Rosenberg, J. (2014). *Google: How Google works.* Grand Central Publishing.

Senge, P. M. (2006). *The fifth discipline: The art and practice of the learning organization.* Doubleday/Currency.

Shokri-Ghasabeh, M., & Chileshe, N. (2014). Knowledge management: Barriers to capturing lessons learned from Australian construction contractors perspective. *Construction Innovation, 14*(1), 108-134. https://doi.org/10.1108/ci-06-2013-0026

Sulistiyani, E., & Tyas, S. H. Y. (2022). What is the measurement of the IT project success? *Procedia Computer Science, 197,* 282-289. https://doi.org/10.1016/j.procs.2021.12.142

Sweller, J. (1988). Cognitive load during problem solving: Effects on learning. *Cognitive Science, 12*(2), 257-285. https://doi.org/10.1207/s15516709cog1202_4

Thomas, K. W., & Velthouse, B. A. (1990). Cognitive elements of empowerment: An "interpretive" model of intrinsic task motivation. *Academy of Management Review, 15*(4), 666-681. https://doi.org/10.5465/amr.1990.4310926

Tiedeman, M. J. (1990). Post-mortems-methodology and experiences. *IEEE Journal on Selected Areas in Communications, 8*(2), 176-180. https://doi.org/10.1109/49.46869

Trienekens, J., & Kusters, R. (2014). Structuring software measurement - metrication in the context of feedback loops. *International Conference on Enterprise Information Systems,* 129-136. https://doi.org/10.5220/0004811401290136

Turner, J. R., & Müller, R. (2005). The project manager's leadership style as a success factor on projects: A literature review. *Project Management Journal, 36*(2), 49-61. https://doi.org/10.1177/875697280503600206

Tversky, A., & Kahneman, D. (1974). Judgment under uncertainty: Heuristics and biases. *Science, 185*(4157), 1124-1131. https://www.jstor.org/stable/1738360

Vaughan, D. (2016). *The Challenger launch decision: Risky technology, culture, and deviance at NASA* (Enlarged). The University of Chicago Press.

Williams, T. (2008). How do organizations learn lessons from projects—and do they? *IEEE Transactions on Engineering Management, 55*(2), 248-266. https://doi.org/10.1109/tem.2007.912920

Yukl, G. A. (2012). *Leadership in organizations* (8th ed.). Pearson Education, Inc.

About the Author

Dr. Joshua Cunio, NPPQ, PMP, is the Managing Director of P3M Strategies LLC, a consulting firm specializing in project, program, and portfolio management, and PILL Framework LLC, where he developed the groundbreaking Project Integrated Lessons Learned (PILL) Framework™. A recognized expert in the field, Dr. Cunio's research focuses on advancing project management practices, exploring causality in project outcomes, and enhancing performance metrics across project, program, and portfolio management.

Dr. Cunio's work bridges the gap between theory and practice, delivering actionable insights that benefit both academia and industry. He is committed to fostering continuous improvement and innovation within the project management discipline.

Dr. Cunio holds a Doctor of Business Administration with a specialization in Project Management from National University, a Master of Science in Project Management from Post University, a Graduate Diploma in Project Portfolio Management from the Institute of Project Management (Sydney, Australia), and a Bachelor of Science in Criminal Justice from California Coast University. In addition, he holds numerous certifications in project and business management, reflecting his dedication to professional excellence and lifelong learning.

www.ingramcontent.com/pod-product-compliance
Lightning Source LLC
Chambersburg PA
CBHW041006210326
41597CB00006B/150